RELATIONSHIP BOOK
FOR NEW COUPLES

Relationship Book for New Couples

Proven Strategies to Nurture Your Connection and Build a Long-Lasting Bond

MEGAN LUNDGREN, LMFT

ROCKRIDGE PRESS

For general information on our other products and services or to obtain technical support, please contact our Customer Care Department within the United States at (866) 744-2665, or outside the United States at (510) 253-0500.

Rockridge Press publishes its books in a variety of electronic and print formats. Some content that appears in print may not be available in electronic books, and vice versa.

Interior and Cover Designer: Brieanna Felschow
Art Producer: Sara Feinstein
Editor: Crystal Nero
Production Editor: Emily Sheehan
Production Manager: Michael Kay
Illustrations used under license from Shutterstock.com.
Author photo courtesy of Daniel Lundgren.

ISBN: Print 978-1-64876-807-1 | eBook 978-1-64876-233-8
R1

FOR DANIEL, THE
LOVE OF MY LIFE.

CONTENTS

viii   INTRODUCTION

1   PART 1 HONORING OUR RELATIONSHIP:
     A CELEBRATION OF COMMITMENT

3   Chapter 1: Who We Are

21   Chapter 2: Where We're Coming From

37   Chapter 3: Our Beliefs and Values

51   PART 2 STRENGTHENING OUR BOND:
     RELATIONSHIP SKILLS

53   Chapter 4: Communication

73   Chapter 5: Closeness

91   Chapter 6: Conflict

109   PART 3 BUILDING OUR FUTURE:
      TOOLS FOR LOOKING AHEAD

111   Chapter 7: Finances and Careers

127   Chapter 8: Family Beyond Us Two

143   Chapter 9: Making It Last

152   RESOURCES

153   REFERENCES

156   INDEX

INTRODUCTION

Congratulations! You've decided to take your relationship to the next level and commit to your partner. Relationships are one of the most important parts of life, and yours is heading toward new depths. You know that relationships grow when they are given nurturing attention, and you are choosing to read a resource that provides research-based tools to help your relationship flourish.

My name is Megan Lundgren, and I'm a licensed marriage and family therapist based in Monrovia, California. For the past 10 years, I have directed Relationships for Better, a therapy private practice focused on helping couples thrive. My colleagues and I are lifelong students of positive relationship psychology—we want to understand the beliefs, attitudes, and behaviors that promote healthy, satisfying, and committed relationships. Through therapy, we equip couples with the tools that help them achieve healthy, lasting intimacy.

In this book, you and your partner will practice evidence-based therapeutic strategies that will enhance the quality of your relationship. Why not make a *good* relationship *great*? Your decision to learn essential relationship skills now will help your partnership thrive. If you're currently experiencing challenges, this book will help you get un-stuck through adaptive relationship skills. If you don't have any major stressors, it will help you build a firm foundation for your newly committed relationship.

This book is for all kinds of newly committed couples—whether you are recently engaged, moving in together, renewing your vows, or preparing for another life milestone. You'll get the most out of it by reading and completing the exercises in this book together. So get ready to cozy up to your partner with a good book!

In part 1, Honoring Our Relationship: A Celebration of Commitment, you and your partner will identify and maximize the unique aspects of your relationship. By building on strengths and values that are unique to you, your beloved partner, and the relationship you've created together, you'll amplify your relationship's potential exponentially.

In part 2, Strengthening Our Bond: Relationship Skills, you and your partner will learn key skills for intimacy. This portion of the book offers evidence-based approaches for addressing the three Cs: communication, closeness, and conflict.

In part 3, Building Our Future: Tools for Looking Ahead, you and your partner will expand on your relationship exploration in part 1 with the key skills learned in part 2, and you'll look ahead to set important goals for your relationship's future.

Throughout this book, you'll find stories of couples who demonstrate the principles and strategies outlined. The names and scenarios are not a depiction of any current or former clients of my therapy practice. While these narratives are authentic reflections of the dynamics commonly experienced in relationship therapy practices, the identities and stories of all my clients remain completely confidential.

Ultimately, I hope that, by reading this book together, you and your partner will have the important conversations that connected and committed relationships are built on. We all want to be known and loved, and the intimate sharing you'll learn in this book is one path toward that.

PART 1

Honoring Our Relationship: A Celebration of Commitment

Let's begin by helping you honor your relationship as it is now, understand where you and your partner are coming from, and get to know each other more deeply. What defines your current relationship? You'll soon find out!

CHAPTER 1

Who We Are

In this chapter, you and your partner will explore your individual identities while also considering the unique identity of your shared relationship. The special qualities that define your relationship will take shape as you work toward understanding yourselves, each other, and the commitment you are making together. This is a key step toward maturity in your relationship.

Us as Individuals

Since you have decided to merge your lives, it might seem counterintuitive to celebrate the differences between you and your partner. But individual identities are a foundation of strong relationships, and learning to appreciate the differences between the two of you will stretch and strengthen your love for each other as distinct, separate beings.

> *"Love rests on two pillars: surrender and autonomy. Our need for togetherness exists alongside our need for separateness.*
>
> *One does not exist without the other. With too much distance, there can be no connection. But too much merging eradicates the separateness of two distinct individuals. Then there is nothing more to transcend, no bridge to walk on, no one to visit on the other side, no other internal world to enter."*
>
> —*Psychologist Esther Perel*

The unique qualities that you and your partner each embody were shaped by many things, including your families of origin, cultural backgrounds, and personalities. So while you may feel as though you know your partner completely, there are always new discoveries to celebrate.

In *The Seven Principles for Making Marriage Work*, famed marriage researcher John Gottman summarizes years of relationship research with this reflection: "Happy marriages are based on a deep friendship." Gottman suggests that couples who are friends "tend to know each other intimately—they are well versed in each other's likes, dislikes, personality quirks, hopes, and dreams." Satisfying intimacy comes from authentic connection between two separate and unique people.

In the classic romantic comedy *Runaway Bride*, Maggie (Julia Roberts) repeatedly leaves grooms at the altar and ends up being ridiculed by the press.

A news reporter asks each rejected groom: "How does Maggie like her eggs?" To his surprise, each fiancé separately replies that Maggie likes her eggs the same way they like their eggs.

The reporter quips to Maggie, "With the priest, you wanted scrambled. With the deadhead, it was fried; with the other guy, it was poached; now, it's egg whites only."

"That is called changing your mind," Maggie replies, defensive.

The reporter retorts, "No, that's called not having a mind of your own."

Maggie impulsively ran away from intimacy because satisfying relationships require that both partners have a sense of their separate identities. Knowing your own preferences, wants, and needs will allow your partner to fully know and love you. In other words, to love another person, you must first know and love yourself.

Getting to Know Each Other

Knowing yourself is the essential step before you can authentically share yourself with another person. Individuals who cultivate a greater degree of identity development tend to experience higher levels of intimacy in their relationships. But how can your partner truly know you unless you've created opportunities for vulnerable reflections?

One of the core practices in creating satisfying and lasting relationships is asking open-ended questions. Questions without a simple "yes" or "no" answer invite deep reflection and storytelling, bringing more intimate conversations into your relationship.

Questions to Deepen Your Relationship

In this reflection exercise, you'll ask each other questions to learn about the particular people, desires, and thoughts that have shaped your individual identities. By sharing personal feelings and listening attentively to each other, you'll demonstrate respect and care for your partner's meaningful life experiences while also nurturing a sense of friendship.

Find a comfortable, private spot to settle in with your partner, and set aside at least an hour for this exercise. Take turns answering the questions, and make sure each person has ample time to share. If you need more time, arrange another time to meet again.

1. Who are the people who have most influenced your life?

2. What were the traditions or cultural experiences that were important to you as a child?

3. When in your life have you felt most relaxed and at ease?

4. Where would you go, if you could go anywhere?

5. What is your ideal day? Describe activities, foods, and the environment around you.

6. Where do you go when you need support?

7. What music, movie, or art is most meaningful to you?

8. What books, classes, or speakers have changed your life?

9. What is a challenge you had to overcome? How did you overcome it?

10. What are the beliefs and values that are most important in your life?

Just for Fun: Two Truths and a Lie

Novel experiences and learning quirky factoids are all part of the fun of getting to know your partner. Kick back with them and share two lighthearted truths . . . and one lie. See if your partner can catch your lie.

E X A M P L E :

I once saw Tom Hanks at Starbucks. I am mildly allergic to strawberries. And I was born with an extra toe.

Our Love Styles

Ancient Greeks demonstrated their respect for love through language: Love was categorized with a multitude of terms, each with different meanings. Though modern English speakers generalize the experience of "love" into a single word, the couples I work with in therapy often find it easier to connect with their partner when they communicate specifically about the kinds of love they experience in their relationship. So what does "I love you" mean to you and your partner?

From the list below, reflect on the three love styles that best reflect the kind of love you currently experience with your partner. Note similarities and differences between the three love styles you each choose.

Eros: Sexual, passionate, romantic love

Phileo: Deep friendship

Ludus: Playful flirtatious, teasing, and fun love

Agape: Altruistic, self-sacrificial love that is loyal and committed, sometimes referred to as divine love

Pragma: Practical, dutiful love built on responsibility and shared goals

Storge: Affectionate, familial love

Us as a Couple

Each relationship has a unique identity. Pioneer of family therapy Carl Whitaker once reflected, "You know, as much as I would miss Muriel [his wife of 50 years] if she were to die, I would miss much more what we are together." Psychologist Terry Hargrave refers to this quality as "us-ness," the identity of the relationship, separate from the identity of each individual participant.

It's essential to understand and nurture your relationship with your partner as an entity of its own. Rather than simply considering what's best for you both as individuals, identify which decisions best serve the relationship that you both love. Regularly asking, "What's best for our relationship?" will guide you and your partner toward a healthy partnership.

Understanding Us

It's important to see, know, and honor your unique relationship's identity. Discuss the following questions with your partner:

1. What is the personality of our relationship? Is our relationship introverted or extroverted? Is our relationship analytical or emotional? Cautious or adventurous?

2. What are the common interests of our relationship?

3. Which beliefs and values are shared in our relationship?

4. How would others describe our relationship?

5. What are the quirks of our relationship?

6. What goals are shared in our relationship?

NURTURING "US-NESS"

Taylor and Leslie began couples therapy because they felt like small issues erupted into major conflicts.

"For example," Taylor confided, "every Friday night, we get into an argument. I usually want to get out of the house and go to dinner, and Leslie usually wants to stay home to watch a documentary."

In the course of the session, it became clear that Leslie and Taylor felt their preferences were at an impasse. The sense of competition between them created defensive walls, limiting their ability to creatively imagine alternative solutions.

Their therapist invited the couple to describe the activities that formed their early dating relationship.

"We went to classes and events at the city college," Leslie said. "And we stayed up for hours talking about our thoughts and debating ideas."

When they delved deeper, Leslie and Taylor realized that neither of them cared much about attending educational events alone, but they shared a genuine interest in learning together and discussing their thoughts. So they decided to nurture the "us" of their relationship by signing up for a current events club and bringing home their favorite takeout afterward to enjoy while discussing the topics.

Taylor and Leslie's "us-ness" includes interests that are unique to their shared relationship and not necessarily direct preferences of their individual identities.

Cooperation Over Conflict

When couples honor their shared relationship, the result is cooperation instead of competition. Hargrave writes, "When two can look at the relationship as an identity in and of itself—the third identity of 'us'—they start to move together in cooperation, not conflict.... It stretches us to grow in ways that would never take place unless we are in the context of another."

Your relationship with your partner may expand both your worldview and your reach. It's important to mindfully consider the impact of your relationship on your life and on the lives of the people around you.

Reflect on the following questions with your partner:

1. What are the ways our relationship has stretched you and helped you grow into a healthier person?

2. What are the ways our relationship benefits the world around you, such as our families, friends, or communities?

3. What are the feelings you are experiencing as you answer these questions?

Our Commitment to Each Other

Clearly communicating your commitment to each other is an essential step in mature relationships. For some people, committing to a relationship means dating exclusively. For others, committing to a relationship means marriage. By specifying the expectations for your shared commitment, you can help prevent confusion and better meet your individual needs.

Commitment Questionnaire

Discuss the following questions with your partner:

1. What is the label or term that you would use to describe your commitment?

2. Is your commitment level:

    a. Private (our relationship status is shared just between us)
    b. Common knowledge (open with friends, family, and acquaintances)
    c. Public (wearing rings, making public demonstrations of affection)

3. How exclusive is your commitment?

4. Does your commitment forbid any particular friendship, communication, or relationship with others?

5. Are there expectations involved in your shared commitment? For example, do you expect your relationship to result in marriage or a family? Do you expect to make major decisions together? Do you expect your partner to remain the same or change in a particular way? Communicate your expectations and offer your partner an opportunity for consent or discussion.

6. Are there objectives in your commitment? Does your relationship have a purpose or goal?

7. Are you open to your partner viewing your:

    a. Social media
    b. Phones
    c. Computers
    d. Finances

8. Is your relationship's commitment tied to a commitment to a particular:

    a. Place or community
    b. Religion
    c. Friend group
    d. Family
    e. Job

9. Are there deal breakers to your commitment to each other? For example, infidelity, addiction, dishonesty, or abuse?

10. Can you name role model relationships that reflect the kind of commitment you would like to have?

THE EX FACTOR

Dakota and Sean walked into the therapy office confused and hurt. Dakota had recently glanced at Sean's friends on social media and noticed that Sean was still friends with an ex. "I didn't do anything wrong; we're just friends," Sean said, aghast. "We've barely even spoken since we broke up." Dakota thought that Sean should un-friend the ex in question. Sean sighed, feeling controlled and defeated.

Through therapy, Dakota and Sean were able to acknowledge that they had entered their relationship with unspoken expectations for their partner. Dakota had expected exes to be deleted from social media and blocked from phones, and Sean expected exes to remain as casual friends.

Sean and Dakota took responsibility for their lack of communication and committed to sharing their hopes for their relationship clearly and often, while providing opportunities for their partner to consent. Through respectful dialogue, they resolved their commitment disagreement and left therapy with a unified vision for the commitment they share in their relationship.

TIP: Unspoken expectations can often turn into resentments. Clarify your expectations now to save your relationship from resentment later. If your partner can't or won't fulfill your expectations, it's better to know as soon as possible.

Try to frame your expectations as requests rather than demands. For example, asking, "Are you willing to end all contact with your ex?" is more respectful than stating, "I expect you to cut off your ex." Respect your partner by allowing them to make a choice for themselves.

Our Love Language

Now that you and your partner have clarified your commitment to each another, let's celebrate the ways you get to communicate your love.

The term "love language" was popularized by Gary Chapman's best-selling book *The Five Love Languages* to describe the general ways that romantic partners express and receive love. Chapman identifies five love languages:

1. Words of affirmation

2. Quality time

3. Receiving gifts

4. Acts of service

5. Physical touch

Your love language is the way that you feel most loved. For example, if your partner's birthday gifts to you are the highlight of your year, you may experience love most effectively through gifts. But the love language that describes how you tend to give love may be different from the love language you prefer to receive. Additionally, the love language you prefer to receive may be different from the love language your partner naturally tends to give.

Consider that your partner's love language is the clearest way to help them receive the message that you love them. While it's not essential to constantly communicate in the love language your partner prefers, it certainly helps build positive appreciation and intimacy in your relationship.

I Felt Loved When ...

Take turns asking your partner to tell you a story about the time they felt most loved in your relationship together.

Does this memory include significant time together, indicating a value of quality time? Were special words spoken? Was a gift given? Was there a sacrificial act of service, such as someone doing a chore or task for you? Was there meaningful physical affection?

Explore together whether these memories of felt love indicate a preference for a particular love language.

Love Language Quiz

Check the two statements that are most true of how you prefer to receive love.

1. ☐ It is meaningful when my partner gives compliments that are specific to me.

2. ☐ I anticipate snuggling and sexual touch with my partner.

3. ☐ I am drawn to my partner when they take care of tasks around the house.

4. ☐ I get excited about spending an entire day with just my partner.

5. ☐ When my partner gives me a special gift, I feel known and loved.

6. ☐ I keep cards that my partner has written to me.

7. ☐ I treasure tokens that my partner has given to me to show they care.

8. ☐ I feel most connected when my partner and I are physically intimate.

9. ☐ I crave vacations with no schedules or interruptions to take me away from my partner.

10. ☐ When my partner chooses to help me instead of relaxing, I know that I'm a priority.

Determining which one or two love languages you prefer to receive:

If you checked 1 or 6, you may prefer verbal affirmation.

If you checked 2 or 8, you may prefer physical touch.

If you checked 3 or 10, you may prefer acts of service.

If you checked 4 or 9, you may prefer quality time.

If you checked 5 and 7, you may prefer receiving gifts.

LOVE TAKES MANY FORMS

Pat and Kai came to the therapy office feeling disconnected.

Pat, an ER nurse, sighed. "I work all day because I love my family. After hours at the hospital, I come home totally drained. All I want to hear, every once in a while, is, 'I appreciate your hard work.' Instead, I get home and Kai has already gone to bed."

"That's frustrating for me too, though!" said Kai. "All I want at the end of the day is a hug or to snuggle you as we fall asleep—but you get home so late from work, and I can't stay awake. Instead, I show my respect for you by making you meals every day, but I'm feeling unappreciated and disconnected."

The good news was that Pat and Kai both genuinely loved each other. The challenge was this: They didn't feel convinced that their partner loved them because the ways they each demonstrated their love were different from the way their partner best received love.

By discussing each of their preferred modes of receiving love, Pat and Kai adapted to their partner's love language: Kai began verbalizing appreciation for Pat's hard work, and Pat found opportunities to more regularly express physical affection to Kai.

Us in Community

Individual identities and relationship identities are made more complete by the addition of communal identities: cultural and social structures that lend relationships a sense of tradition, stability, and support. Community includes the friends, family, neighbors, colleagues, and social groups that can be woven together to create a net that holds individuals and relationships securely in place.

Researcher David Lapp sums up his studies on community support's impact on marriage stability this way: "A marriage is held together not only by the two spouses, but by the web of relationships that surrounds them."

A healthy community is a network of usually reciprocal relationships, in which couples are accepted and holistically served by their communities while they, in turn, accept and serve the community around them.

When couples rely heavily on their partner and no one else, it can put unnecessary pressure on their relationship. But when they root their relationship in a community, they gain support and emotional resilience through the compassion of friends and mentors. They can also find deeper meaning in their relationship, as they look outward to support others. In short, when couples learn to give and receive in communities, those communities help create resilient and mature relationships.

QUESTIONS FOR REFLECTION

1. Name the three people who know you best outside of your partner.
2. Describe the culture in which your relationship currently exists. What are the values of that culture?
3. Are there ethnic identities or traditions that shape the way you approach your relationship with your partner?
4. What are three ways the community that surrounds your relationship can support you in your new commitment?
5. Name three relationship role models: couples in your community who embody characteristics that you strive for in your relationship with your partner.

Kelsey and Hayden sat on the therapy office sofa, beaming. Though Hayden had recently experienced the stress of a health scare, their friends and family had rallied around them and provided meals, babysitting, and comfort. After the test results came back clear, they celebrated not only the relief of renewed health but the confirmation that their relationship is scaffolded by the strong support of a dozen loved ones.

"I remember our wedding day, when our officiant turned to the congregation and asked, 'Will all of you witnessing these promises do all in your power to uphold these two persons in their marriage?'" Hayden reflected. "I know what that means now."

Throughout the therapy process, the therapist heard stories about Hayden and Kelsey's community often. Their relationship seemed to grow resilient and grounded through the support of their loved ones, though often in intangible or indirect ways. For example, though Hayden and Kelsey rarely disclosed their relational conflicts with their family, the Sunday dinners they shared with Kelsey's parents gave them perspective as they witnessed an older couple's marital spats and repair process.

"When my dad puts his hand on my mom's shoulder, I know that he is saying, 'I'm sorry,'" Kelsey said. "It's comforting to see how they make their relationship work, year after year. We want to do things differently in our relationship, of course. But we learn from their relationship, too."

Kelsey and Hayden enjoyed a sense of community through friends and family. Other couples find community in mentors, coworkers, religious communities, cultural institutions, volunteer work, and recreational activities. Community strengthens commitment and adds rich meaning to a relationship's identity.

TIP: Find friends who are also couples. Though each individual in a relationship benefits from friends of their own, couples who are friends with both of you offer living examples of relationship strengths and challenges. By discussing what you both learn from the relationships around you, you can more easily create the kind of relationship you desire.

Couple Check-In

Congrats! You and your partner have celebrated your individual identities, your relationship's identity, and the communal context in which your relationship exists. Your work in developing insight into your relationship will be a firm foundation in your new commitment together.

Take this opportunity to check in with each other. How are you feeling about yourselves and your relationship after discussing the topics and practicing the strategies in this chapter? Listen compassionately and validate your partner's feelings. You each may be experiencing different emotions, so try to understand and accept your partner's experience without judgment.

In the next chapter, we'll explore the family and experiences that shaped the person you are today. As you and your partner understand where you're both coming from, you'll have an even better idea of where you're going in your relationship.

CHAPTER 2

Where We're Coming From

"We do as we have been done by."

–John Bowlby

Your past doesn't dictate the present, but it does inform the present. There's a reason nearly every relationship therapist routinely says, "Tell me about your family." Experiences with family members, peers, authority figures, and previous relationships are all emotionally significant.

Neuropsychology findings suggest that emotionally impactful experiences in relationships, particularly in childhood, form neural pathways in the brain. Neural pathways are like well-worn highways that pave the way for how we're prone to interpret future events. For example, if a child experienced an overwhelming sense of care and safety in their childhood home, that child's brain forms a neural pathway for love and safety. Later in life, that neural pathway may allow them to be more likely to trust a partner or give them the benefit of the doubt.

In this chapter, we'll explore how your past experiences may impact your relationship with your partner, for better or for worse.

The Past and Present

As you establish your commitment to each other, it's important to talk to your partner about patterns of behavior and treatment that were norms in your childhood, your previous relationships, and your parents' relationship. Though you can't control the past, you can understand how norms set in prior experiences might affect you now. If you experienced positive past relationships, you may be able to borrow tools and strategies from those success stories. If you experienced challenging past relationships, this chapter will help you avoid projecting those experiences onto your current relationship.

Our Families of Origin

The term "family of origin" refers to the small unit of people who cared for you when you were young. Your family of origin may be different from your biological family or your broader community. For some people, their biological or adoptive parents and siblings are their family of origin. For others, it may be family members through marriage or aunts, uncles, or grandparents.

Your family of origin taught you the basics of relationships: how to interact with the people close to you. Childhood neural pathways are heavily influenced by family or caregiver relationships. Based on whether your family of origin demonstrated love, you learned to internally answer the question, "Am I loved?" Similarly, based on the degree of security or predictability of your family of origin, you learned to internally answer the question, "Am I safe?"

These experiences form the basis for your thought patterns and behavior at an early age. The lessons learned in childhood can last a lifetime and have dramatic effects on the relationship you share with your partner today.

Discovering Families of Origin

Exploring the families of origin in which you and your partner were raised is crucial to understanding the patterns and dynamics of your current relationship. Here, we'll identify some of the relationship structures that were commonplace in your childhood homes and during your formative years.

It's important to note that your family of origin doesn't necessarily predict the kind of relationship you have with your partner. Though people who experienced positive family relationships often opt to replicate the family relationship styles modeled to them, individuals who experienced distressing family relationships may actively avoid repeating their family's dynamics, choosing a vastly different relational approach. Discussing your family of origin is just the beginning—it lays the groundwork for understanding why your relationship functions the way it does.

Olson's Circumplex Model, supported by more than 1,000 studies over the past 30 years, indicates that family systems function in terms of two dimensions: adaptability (the ways in which families handle changing circumstances) and cohesiveness (the degree to which families connect).

ADAPTABILITY
Rigid versus Chaotic
Rigid ↔ Structured ↔ Flexible ↔ Chaotic

COHESIVENESS
Enmeshed versus Disengaged
Enmeshed ↔ Connected ↔ Separated ↔ Disengaged

My Family's Adaptivity

From the options below, circle which family structure relating to adaptivity best reflects your household as a child. Tell your partner a story about how your family handled rules or change when you were growing up.

Rigid Family: My family had strict rules, authoritarian leadership, and unwavering expectations. (For example, your grades may have been heavily monitored.)

Structured Family: My family had rules with some room for flexibility. (For example, your bedtime and mealtime may have been enforced during the week yet relaxed on the weekends.)

Flexible Family: My family had some rules, but parents were willing to negotiate. (For example, you may have been expected to attend holiday functions but may have been excused from certain other family events.)

Chaotic Family: My family had few rules, and the rules that did exist frequently changed. (For example, your parents may have heavily punished a broken curfew one weekend and then not at all the following weekend.)

QUESTION FOR DISCUSSION

How has your family of origin's adaptive style impacted your relationship? Identify positive or negative ways your family's experiences with expectations and change have shaped the way you approach your relationship with your partner.

SLEEPING ARRANGEMENTS

Ashok and Priya kept apologizing about the seemingly silly content of their conflict that week. "I feel so embarrassed, but we have been fighting all week over our dog," Priya reflected. "I often let the dog jump on our bed and snuggle with us at night. I love those moments, but they make Ashok really angry."

"It's not right," Ashok said defensively. "We decided that our dog would sleep in the dog bed. If we don't set firm boundaries now, the dog will never stop begging to sleep on our bed."

As is often the case with minor conflicts, this fight wasn't just about the dog. Ashok and Priya's emotional attachments to structured or flexible expectations were related to the norms of their childhood homes. Though both Ashok and Priya grew up in strict households, their reactions to those environments varied: Ashok respected the predictability and routine that he experienced in his childhood home and sought to replicate that experience in his relationship with Priya, while Priya resented that rules seemed to come before relationship in her family of origin.

As Priya and Ashok shared, their empathy for each other widened. They were able to understand their partner's emotional rationale, without invalidating their own experiences. Priya understood why Ashok valued consistency, and Ashok understood why Priya valued connection. Mutual understanding paved the way for mutual respect. As it turned out, collaborative problem-solving wasn't as hard once they each took responsibility for how their past impacted their present emotions.

My Family's Cohesiveness

As you read the descriptions below, identify which family structure relating to cohesiveness best reflects your household as a child. Tell your partner a story of how your family experienced distance or connection when you were growing up.

Enmeshed Family: My family had few boundaries. They were heavily involved in one another's lives. (For example, your parents may have frequently involved themselves in your friendships when you were a teenager.)

Connected Family: My family was generally involved, but we enjoyed our privacy. (For example, your parents may have attended your events or activities but excused themselves from participating in your personal life.)

Separated Family: My family was unaware of what I was doing in my personal time. (For example, your parents may not have been aware of your personal hobbies or interests.)

Disengaged Family: My family lived disconnected lives, like roommates or business partners. (For example, your parents may have rarely asked questions or demonstrated curiosity.)

QUESTION FOR DISCUSSION

How has your family of origin's cohesiveness style impacted your relationship? Identify positive or negative ways your family's experiences with connection or disconnection have shaped the way you approach your relationship with your partner.

ALL IN THE FAMILY

Maria and Jordan were exhausted. Between wedding planning, work, and graduate school, they hardly had time to connect with each other. Maria spent every weekend with her family, decompressing by her parents' pool in hopes of managing her stress, and Jordan felt disconnected.

"I imagined engagement being a romantic time in our relationship, but I feel like Maria's relationship is mainly with her parents," Jordan revealed. "I hardly see her anymore."

Maria was confused; she loved her parents and didn't understand why Jordan wouldn't want her to be close to them.

"My mom has been helpful with every step of wedding planning," Maria responded. "She and I talk about it every single day—I'm surprised you're not grateful to her. And my dad has been such an incredible emotional support. I don't know where I would be without him."

"I want you to be happy, Maria," Jordan said. "I just don't feel like you and your parents are leaving any room for me."

In the course of therapy, Maria learned to build healthy coping mechanisms to manage stress, decreasing her perceived need to depend on her family. Though she remained connected with her parents, Maria recognized that she had prioritized her family's emotional closeness above personal and relational development. Maria's parents weren't always understanding of her decision to spend less time at home, but Maria learned how to tolerate their discomfort. Differentiating herself from family allowed Maria to mature, witness her capabilities, and chart a course for her next chapter.

Differentiating Families of Origin

You are not the direct by-product of your family of origin. Though it may have significantly impacted your thoughts and behaviors in early childhood, knowing your family of origin gives you the power to choose to model your relationship with your partner in similar or different ways.

> **TIP:** Do you find it difficult to talk about your parents or care-givers because you don't want to place blame? Identifying the emotional and behavioral patterns of your family of origin is simply naming the facts. Once you've identified childhood patterns, you can decide which ones are beneficial to hold on to and which are better to let go of. Choosing a different relational approach than your family doesn't necessarily require blame or judgment.

Name at least one way in which your current relationship style (communication patterns, norms for affectionate behaviors, structure, or flexibility) is different from that of your family of origin.

QUESTION FOR DISCUSSION

Discuss this with your partner, each affirming the ways you have differentiated or defined yourself separately from the family in which you were raised.

Attachment Theory

Now that you've identified your family of origin's structure and the way that informs your current relationship, let's focus on the way your family of origin has the greatest impact on your current relationship: attachment style.

Attachment theory is a concept developed in 1958 by John Bowlby, whose research suggests that infants have a universal need to seek close contact with their caregiver when under stress. According to Bowlby, the degree of security that an infant or child feels with their caregiver may impact the degree of stress, trust, and attachment or emotional bond they experience later in life. The manner in which you attached to your family of origin as a child can significantly impact your ability to trust and connect to your relationship with your partner today.

Most people have varying aspects of each of the four primary attachment styles, and they can change over time. For instance, individuals who were neglected by a caregiver can have a "corrective experience" of a partner caring for them with consistency and trustworthiness, thus influencing their current attachment style. Others may need professional assistance through therapy to address the unmet needs and emotional harm inflicted through a damaging relationship with a caregiver. Determining your attachment style via the quiz below can help you identify potential relational issues and understand the support you may need to create a successful relationship.

Attachment Quiz

Check each statement that honestly reflects your feelings and internal attitudes, particularly in your relationship with your partner. You will likely check statements in multiple categories, but the category with the most checks is an indicator of your primary attachment style.

Secure Attachment Style

☐ I feel natural and comfortable expressing my feelings and needs to my partner.

☐ I am effective at communicating my needs to my partner.

☐ I am willing to compromise with my partner.

☐ I can express emotions effectively, without shutting down or exploding.

☐ I am comfortable receiving affection from my partner and feel safe doing so.

☐ I am at ease when I am alone, and I am at ease when I am with my partner.

☐ I work hard to solve problems in relationships without attacking my partner.

☐ I have ups and downs, but I am generally resilient.

Anxious Preoccupied Attachment Style

- ☐ I am anxious about the security of my relationship.
- ☐ I recognize that I am needy, possessive, jealous, or obsessive in my relationship with my partner.
- ☐ I am cautious to the point of being pessimistic in my relationship with my partner.
- ☐ I need frequent reminders that I am loved.
- ☐ I feel insecure if my partner doesn't validate me often.
- ☐ I experience conflict in my relationship when I need to feel accepted or reassured.
- ☐ I am uncomfortable spending too much time alone.
- ☐ I have a history of turbulent relationships.

Dismissive Avoidant Attachment Style

- ☐ I am self-sufficient. I prefer to be independent.
- ☐ I have a difficult time with emotional intimacy with my partner.
- ☐ I crave freedom; I like to make my own choices.
- ☐ I have commitments that come before my relationship, such as work.
- ☐ I don't feel like I need a relationship.
- ☐ I have a number of acquaintances, though I lack close friendships.
- ☐ I am somewhat annoyed by emotional conversations in relationships.
- ☐ I feel hesitant with commitment; I prefer autonomy and control.

Fearful Avoidant Attachment Style

- ☐ I am insecure and doubt that people like me.
- ☐ I am hesitant to rely on others.
- ☐ I am confused: I both desire and fear intimacy.

☐ I have experienced abuse, neglect, parental addiction, or the traumatic loss of a loved one.

☐ I push other people away and find it difficult to remain close with others.

☐ I find it easy to imagine my relationship falling apart, even though it seems stable.

☐ I get suspicious that my partner is insincere even though I don't have reasons for mistrust.

☐ I feel safest when I am independent.

If you answered mainly in the Secure Attachment Style:

- Today, you may feel confident in your relationship with your partner. You may feel like you can trust your partner and enjoy independence while allowing your partner independence as well. You may easily express love and reach out for support.

- Questions for reflection: Early in life, did you feel happy to be with your caregiver but also confident to explore the world on your own? Or was there another personal relationship that provided you with a sense of safety?

- Plan for action: Consider an outward lens. Since you experience security in your relationship with your partner, consider ways in which you can support your partner if they have a different attachment style.

If you answered mainly in the Anxious Preoccupied Attachment Style:

- Today, you may experience significant needs for emotional intimacy, approval, and reassurance in your relationship.

- Questions for reflection: Early in life, did you experience a caregiver's emotional absence? Did you feel unsure of whether your needs would be met?

- Plan for action: Consider working through the roots of anxiety in therapy, moving from "emotional hunger" in your relationship to a true emotional bond.

If you answered mainly in the Dismissive Avoidant Attachment Style:

- Today, you may experience discomfort with emotional intimacy and feel reluctant to trust your partner.

- Questions for reflection: Early in life, did you experience absence from a caregiver? Did you feel rejected from your family of origin or peers at pivotal points in development?

- Plan for action: Consider working through challenges with trust in therapy, learning to become open to vulnerable connection with your partner.

If you answered mainly in the Fearful Avoidant Attachment Style:

- Today, you may experience confusion in your relationship, desiring intimacy and yet pushing your partner away.

- Questions for reflection: Early in life, did you experience inconsistent security and connectedness with your family of origin? Were your caregivers hot and cold in their relationship with you?

- Plan for action: Consider working with a therapist to process and organize childhood experiences, clarifying your current needs and desires in your relationship with your partner.

Knowing your attachment style is key to understanding your baseline—what feels most natural to you in your relationship. With this awareness, you can begin to responsibly address the underlying emotional needs you may be trying to meet through your relationship with your partner. Therapy can give you added support to acknowledge past pains and move toward a bright future.

MENDING CHILDHOOD WOUNDS

Alex and Sage were the image of a happy, secure couple. They got together in college and had been inseparable ever since. But in the context of therapy, it became clear that anxiety lived under the surface of their pristine relationship.

Alex required reassurance from Sage on a daily basis, feeling restless and insecure if Sage didn't provide constant compliments and praise. Doubting every small decision, Alex texted Sage for approval and reassurance. When Sage expressed feeling tired of this, Alex eagerly sought to please by reducing the texts but was no less anxious, merely suppressing those feelings from Sage for fear of losing the relationship.

An exploration of Alex's childhood uncovered an experience of distant caregivers and few other social supports. Alex's brain had learned to prioritize relational security above all else, becoming hypervigilant to minimize potential risks to a prized relationship.

Alex eventually learned to compassionately tend to childhood wounds and discern personal preferences and desires, realizing his constant quest for security had robbed him of the question, "What do I want?" Conflicts followed, but each conflict opened doors to a more fulfilling relationship for both partners. Ultimately, Alex and Sage's hard work earned them a more authentic and intimate relationship in which commitment was a thoughtful choice, rather than insurance against abandonment.

Addressing Unhealthy Attachments

Unhealthy attachments can occur in relationships with caregivers, partners, friends, mentors— even therapists! Consider the following symptoms of an unhealthy attachment, circling any that resonate with a current adult relationship in your life:

- I am in a one-sided relationship, where one person depends on the other to meet all of their needs.

- I cover up another person's problems and isolate from my support system.

- I feel trapped in a relationship with another person.

- I avoid conflicts and keep quiet.

- I am abused, threatened, or mistreated.

- I am shamed, dismissed, or treated as "less than" another person.

- I am monitored, spied on, or controlled in decisions.

- I am told that others do not like me or will think I'm crazy.

If you circled any of the symptoms of unhealthy attachment above, seek the assistance of a therapist, social worker, or domestic violence center to remove yourself from the unhealthy relationship and seek personal safety.

Couple Check-In

Breaking the patterns of unhealthy attachments is not only possible; it's necessary. Once you are free from the bounds of an unhealthy attachment, the healing begins.

In the next chapter, you will explore the beliefs and values that are most important to you and discover how to integrate those into your relationship with your partner.

CHAPTER 3

Our Beliefs and Values

Do you and your partner believe that the same things in life are important? Identifying common ground in your beliefs and values is essential when forming a healthy relationship commitment.

Finding Common Ground

I've observed that couples who share values enjoy higher relationship satisfaction and individual well-being than those who do not. Values are what you believe is important and meaningful in life, creating the foundation of how you intend to live. They reflect things like your personal identity, relational identity (for example, culture or family of origin), spiritual beliefs, and moral code.

According to a study by John Gottman, relationships thrive when couples focus on "creating an inner life together—a culture rich with symbols and rituals, and an appreciation of your roles and goals that link you, that lead you to understand what it means to be part of the family you have become." Your life decisions are oriented around your values. What are the morals and values that you want to keep central in your newly committed relationship?

Morals and Values

Using the list below, circle five values that are very important to you. Have your partner identify five values that are important to them as well. Discuss similarities and differences in the values you choose. Are there ways your relationship helps you embody your chosen values?

Adventure	Frugality	Legacy	Respect
Authenticity	Generosity	Love	Rest
Community	Gratitude	Loyalty	Security
Compassion	Growth	Mercy	Self-Control
Contentment	Health	Optimism	Simplicity
Cooperation	Honesty	Patience	Spirituality
Creativity	Hospitality	Peace	Tradition
Education	Joy	Perseverance	Trust
Faith	Justice	Playfulness	Wealth
Family	Kindness	Progress	Wisdom
Friendship	Leadership	Relationships	

If your values seem to clash with your partner's, take this as an opportunity to clarify them. For example, if one partner values progress and the other partner values stability, tell each other the stories that led to the development of these values. Intimacy breeds empathy—if you know your partner deeply, you're more likely to empathize with their values.

Empathizing with your partner's values doesn't necessarily mean you agree with those values. It's important to identify and communicate your boundaries. If you and your partner have fundamental differences in key values and aren't able to find a compromise, it's essential to consider how this could affect the future of your commitment. Opting for the support of a skilled therapist may assist you both in navigating the murky waters of value differences.

QUESTION FOR DISCUSSION

How you and your partner spend time and money may be indicators of current values. Do your intended values align with your current use of time or money? Is there an opportunity to shift your use of time or money to live more in alignment with your values?

Religion and Spirituality

Spiritual beliefs and religious traditions can impact your relationship's happiness. An extensive study of 21,501 couples found that 89 percent of couples who reported that they were happy in their relationship indicated that they experienced "satisfaction and agreement with how spiritual values and beliefs are expressed" within it.

Research also suggests that when dating couples participate in religious activities together, the quality of their relationship may benefit. According to the Pew Research Center, nearly half of all married couples say that sharing religious beliefs is "very important" for a successful marriage, though couples from the same religion hold this stance significantly more strongly than intra-religious couples.

Discussing spiritual beliefs or religious traditions with your partner can help you decide whether to integrate faith into your relationship.

1. Are spiritual beliefs an important element of commitment in our relationship?
2. Do you feel that we agree or disagree about spiritual beliefs in our relationship? Do differences in spiritual beliefs cause tension or apprehension in our relationship?
3. How has your culture or family of origin informed your spiritual beliefs?
4. Do you currently participate in a religious community or engage in religious traditions? If yes:

   - Is it important to you that I participate with you in these activities?
   - Is it important that potential future children share with you in these activities?

FINDING COMMON SPIRITUAL GROUND

Justice and Alexis found their therapist through Justice's pastor. Though Justice and Alexis initially thought they were compatible due to their devout Christian faith, certain differences became more apparent as their relationship became more committed: Justice's lifelong membership in the Mennonite Church seemed at odds with Alexis's passionate involvement in a large, nondenominational church. In therapy, they both expressed a feeling of discomfort that their partner wasn't comfortable leaving their congregation to join them in shared worship and fellowship.

One of the first things the therapist did was identify common beliefs that both partners saw as essential. Justice and Alexis created a Venn diagram with quite a large center of shared essential beliefs.

Next, the therapist determined the feelings of pain that Justice and Alexis felt when acknowledging their different Christian traditions.

"I feel alone," Justice confessed. "I don't want us to go to different services on a constant basis. I want to introduce Alexis to my friends and mentors."

"I can understand that," Alexis remarked. "I feel lonely, too. I don't know anything about the Mennonite Church, and I feel like an outsider."

By naming the specific pain surrounding their discomfort, Alexis and Justice were able to focus on resolving their feelings of being alone. Justice introduced Alexis to the congregation, and Alexis set up meetings with Justice's pastor to learn more about Mennonite doctrine and traditions. Eventually, Alexis joined Justice at Sunday services, while Justice participated in a weekly small group through Alexis's church. Ultimately, what seemed to matter most to Alexis and Justice was that they were included and involved in each other's lives. Through these shared theological discussions and an expanding network of social support, the couple laid the foundation for the faith-centered relationship they both desired.

Politics

On online dating websites, people may evaluate potential partners more positively or be more likely to reach out if they have similar political leanings. Research shows that modern couples often choose a potential partner based in part on political beliefs, resulting in unified political beliefs within households. Though this unification often lends itself to a sense of harmony, relationships with varied perspectives can sometimes create opportunities for deeper understanding of values underlying a political stance, as well as further opportunities for learning from alternative sources.

No matter how unified or diverse your values might be, the topic of politics can still cause debate for couples. Try to approach discussions about political beliefs with respect and curiosity— sincerely listen to your partner's reflections, and dig for understanding.

1. How do you choose to vote for a particular party, political candidate, or ballot measure? What is the process that determines your vote?
2. What key principles or values create the foundation for your vote?
3. Does your vote reflect your particular life experiences, religious beliefs, or ethnic/cultural background?
4. Are there particular feelings that drive your voting preferences—for example, fear or hope?

A VOTE FOR CURIOSITY

"Either you are with me or you are against me!" Victoria said, firmly.

"I guess I'm against you then," Shayne replied sarcastically.

An election was nearing, and Victoria and Shayne were feeling the tension of their decision to vote for different political parties.

"Let's find new language to describe the values and beliefs at the root of your voting convictions," their therapist suggested. "It may help you two empathize or understand each other. Condescension and critique are going to shut down the conversation, so let's get curious instead. To get an honest reflection out of your partner, they need to know that you're not looking to judge them—you're trying to understand them. Are you two ready to try to understand each other?"

Victoria and Shayne nodded.

"I feel that voting in favor of legalizing immigration is a proud part of my heritage, since I come from a family of immigrants," Victoria began. "I can't imagine voting in a way that might hurt the people who have cared for me all my life."

"That makes sense," Shayne reflected. "It's actually similar to why I vote pro-life. I feel like it's a tribute to my brother with Down syndrome. I guess we're both fiercely loyal to our families."

Their therapist affirmed the couple's ability to share their feelings and convictions in a way that both partners could understand and respect. Nonjudgmental curiosity made way for honest insight in their relationship.

> **TIP:** Name a personally transformative experience, whether through meaningful relationships or a memorable learning event, that resulted in a particular voting decision.

Culture

Where did you grow up? What is your family's racial or ethnic background? How has the color of your skin impacted your life experiences? Naming the importance of cultural heritages has always been important in relationships, but these discussions may take on fresh importance as interracial and interethnic relationships grow more common across the United States. Even if you and your partner have the same general ethnic or racial background, consider discussing how cultural differences can vary across socioeconomic or geographical landscapes.

QUESTIONS FOR DISCUSSION

1. What do family relationships look like in your culture?
2. Are particular roles assigned by gender in your culture?
3. Are you expecting your relationship to fulfill any culturally relevant roles? For example, if women commonly stay at home in early parenthood while partners financially provide for the family, would that be expected in your relationship?
4. Are there cultural expectations around committing to an individual from a similar background?
5. What are cultural expectations based on gender?
6. Are there expectations for particular birth orders? For example, were you expected to fulfill any particular roles as an oldest, middle, youngest, or only child?
7. Do cultural expectations vary if someone is single, dating, married, or a parent?

A SHARED PATH TO THE FUTURE

"My mother wants me to be with someone from our small town in Mexico," Blanca said, glancing nervously at her boyfriend, Clarke, who comes from an Irish-American family. "She envisions me speaking Spanish in the home like we did, making tamales every Christmas, and dancing at a quinceañera for a granddaughter someday."

Clarke felt defeated. Didn't Blanca's mother care that she was already in a relationship?

Two keys to therapy success are insight and motivation—and, fortunately, Blanca and Clarke had both. Over the course of therapy, Blanca determined that she had focused so much energy on honoring her mother that she hadn't paused to ask herself what she wanted for her own future.

"I want to pass on my cultural heritage to the next generation if we have kids," Blanca shared one day in session. "I know that there is a dual-immersion Spanish-English school down the street; how would you feel about sending our kids there when the time comes?" Clarke was relieved to have a straightforward path toward respecting Blanca's wishes. At the next session, Clarke proudly showed me a language app he had downloaded, with the goal of becoming bilingual.

Over time, Blanca and Clarke became close with a number of inter cultural and interracial couples who understood their relationship's challenges and benefits. One additional reward of Blanca and Clarke's hard work was that their communication skills grew exponentially. Because they didn't come from similar cultural backgrounds, Blanca and Clarke learned not to make assumptions and to proactively communicate expectations and intentions. In the end, they had a rich and fulfilling relationship that was completely their own.

Traditions and Customs

When traditions and customs—like songs, holidays, recipes, and practices—are passed down from one generation to the next, they also often bring with them a sense of belonging and purpose. As you take the next step toward commitment in your relationship, it's important to understand and share the traditions and customs that are important to you both.

QUESTIONS FOR DISCUSSION

1. What holidays did your family celebrate?
2. What food or activities from your family of origin or culture are meaningful to you?
3. How do you hope to spend holidays as your relationship continues?
4. What are the rites of passage in your culture? Are people treated differently at particular ages or after achieving a particular goal or life milestone?
5. Are there meaningful places you are expected to visit?
6. Are there customs that I would be expected not to participate in?
7. Are there customs that may impact our relationship in a particular way?

Practicing the age-old, inherited traditions of your family, culture, or religion may be an important way to honor your heritage and beliefs. But developing new quirky, personalized traditions can help solidify a special sense of belonging in your unique relationship.

Start Something New

Create a new tradition with your partner. Consider using a holiday, birthday, or season for context. Think about which people, foods, music, games, books, activities, religious practices, or aspects of nature might be involved in your relationship's new tradition.

Some examples of odd traditions in my family:

- We sing a song taught by my grandmother, "Tomorrow Will Be Thanksgiving Day," on—you guessed it—the day before Thanksgiving. This tradition is also a race: The first extended family member to call and sing on the day before Thanksgiving wins.

- We use the nylon stockings of a deceased matriarch in our family as our Christmas stockings, filling them with gifts. (The odder the tradition, the better!)

- We make a volcano cake for my son's birthday every year, complete with dry ice smoke. Every birthday has a different theme—this year was ocean-themed—but every cake must include an active volcano.

What meaningful traditions and practices from your family, religion, or culture would you like to integrate into your new commitment with your partner? What oddball traditions would you like to fold into the mix as you establish a special sense of togetherness with your partner?

United Beliefs and Values

While it's important to have individual values and beliefs, it's also important to establish the shared vision of your relationship. What beliefs, values, and objectives will serve as the foundation? How will you use the partnership of your relationship to benefit the world around you?

One of the best ways to identify, celebrate, and challenge yourselves toward shared values is through a mission statement.

On a piece of paper or a whiteboard, create a vision board:

1. On one side, write six total individual personality or character traits for you and your partner (three for each of you).

2. On the other side, write each of your individual values from earlier in this chapter.

3. Reflecting on these sets of words, write a statement that includes four parts:

    a. What you have to offer
    b. What ideals or values you're willing to work toward
    c. In what context
    d. For what purpose

For example, one couple may write:

Because we are both extroverted, gregarious people, we will work toward demonstrating hospitality with our extended family and friends, using our home as a place to build community and meaningful relationships.

Another couple with different personalities and values could write:

We're a dynamic combination: thoughtful and intuitive combined with driven problem-solving. Together, we'll extend mercy to our neighbors by offering emotional support and civic responsibility, in hopes of making our neighborhood a more loving place.

> TIP: Some of the most united and focused couples I've counseled over the years have a funny quirk in common: They sometimes refer to themselves as Team (Last Name). When they have to rally through a tough circumstance, these couples will remind themselves and each other of their shared identity or vision. "C'mon, we can do this! We're Team Chen! We've got this!"

Do you encourage each other to reach important goals? Remind your partner that you make a good team!

Couple Check-In

In this chapter, we explored your individual and relational beliefs and values. You discussed the ways that spiritual beliefs, politics, culture, and race may impact your relationship, considering the ways each of your differences work together for the good of your relationship. Finally, you looked outside of yourselves and created a mission statement that challenges you to work toward meaningful values or goals in your relationship and in the world around you.

Now that you've spent time exploring each other, your pasts, and your relationship's present, it's time to dig into building key skills for strengthening your bond. Get ready to address the three Cs: communication, closeness, and conflict.

PART 2

Strengthening Our Bond: Relationship Skills

What relationship skills are required to make your relationship last? In this section, you'll learn to communicate effectively, thrive in intimacy, and navigate conflict with a sense of purpose. Your relationship's future is based on the foundation you lay today, so let's get to work on building a satisfying relationship for years to come!

CHAPTER 4

Communication

Communication is the oxygen in a relationship—you can't survive without it, but you can breathe easy when you have it.

Communication Is Essential

The most essential skill you can develop when cultivating a healthy and thriving relationship is communication. It's the one thing that will positively impact your relationship on a daily basis, regardless of life circumstance.

While positive communication promotes relational bliss, a 2013 survey of mental health professionals revealed that communication problems are one of the primary causes of divorce. So how do those problems develop? We form our communication patterns in our family of origin, meaning that the way your mom talked to your dad may be the way you're tempted to talk with your partner.

Fortunately, building successful communication in your relationship isn't dependent on what was modeled in your parents' marriage. As the director of a relationship therapy practice, I've learned that practicing responsible, clear, and validating communication is a teachable skill that any couple can learn.

The communication strategies that I share in this chapter focus on practical methods for couples who are eager to take their relationship to the next level.

How to Be a Great Listener

Have you ever felt deeply understood by another person? Chances are, you were validated—in other words, you felt as though the other person recognized and accepted your feelings, thoughts, and behaviors. By validating your partner's perspective, you're saying that their experience makes sense.

One of the best parts about validation is that it doesn't require agreement. To say, "I can understand why you feel the way that you do," or, "I hear you," doesn't necessarily mean, "I agree with you." By accepting your partner's perspective, you're demonstrating that you are each committed to caring for each other in spite of your differences.

Active Listening

Active listening is a tried-and-true technique for establishing positive communication through sensitive listening.

Instead of indulging distractions, interrupting, or reacting emotionally during times of sharing, couples who practice active listening mindfully—and slowly—take turns communicating. The goal is to put your own opinions on hold so that you can listen deeply to your partner's feelings. The benefit? A thriving relationship.

EXERCISE

To practice active listening with your partner, begin by having them share a highlight from their day. Then simply restate what you heard, using your own words. "It sounds like you enjoyed..."

Paraphrasing your partner's reflections lets them know that you were listening intently, which shows love and respect. Reflective listening also provides an opportunity to ensure that you and your partner are on the same page.

Ask your partner to share a "low moment" from their day. After restating their reflection, check for understanding: "Is that right?" Give your partner a chance to clarify, if they want to.

Active listening will help you and your partner feel understood, nurtured, and validated. Use this exercise daily during a meal to provide a firm foundation for communication in your relationship.

Disconnect Digitally

Though technology may be responsible for your nostalgic first swipes, tweets, DMs, or snaps with your partner, it can also be a significant barrier to clear communication.

Before you picture me prying the smartphone out of your hands, know that I'm a fan of modern technology. My objective is simply to help you be an informed consumer of technology who is mindful of its implications for relational communication with your partner.

The first challenge with technology and communication is that the time we spend using it every day can rob our relationships of precious time to communicate. After so much screen time, couples often have little time and energy left in their days for quality communication with each other.

The second challenge with technology is that a significant part of communication is nonverbal. So when partners rely on technology for communication, they often lose the nonverbal cues (facial expressions, gestures, tone) that help decipher the meaning of a message. Couples who use text for emotional conversations leave themselves vulnerable to rampant miscommunication.

Challenge yourself to put down your devices at the same time for 30 minutes every day for a meaningful debrief of the day's highs and lows. This will provide the invaluable opportunity to emotionally connect with your partner. Use those 30 minutes of quality communication to look into your partner's eyes, listen attentively, and celebrate the day's wins and mourn its losses.

Get Curious

Have you ever noticed yourself making assumptions about your partner? You know each other well now that you're at the point of commitment, but like all healthy living things, your partner is constantly developing and changing. In graduate school, one of my old professors used to quip, "I've been married to seven different women." He would then disclose that, really, he had been married to one woman who had changed significantly seven times in the course of their decades-long marriage.

Ask your partner about their preferences, priorities, fantasies, and fears and then listen with respect and gratitude. Getting curious about your partner demonstrates that you are attempting to love them as they are, acknowledging their ability to change. Often, people feel honored when loved ones ask them questions, but if your partner feels uncomfortable with a particular question, don't force them to answer it. Remember to let them know that you are interested in getting to know them so that you can love them even more.

Respect

"Is now a good time to talk, or should we connect at another time?"

"Do you need 10 minutes to wind down after work before we touch base?"

There are many ways to convey respect for your partner. Learning to communicate respect is one of the most essential skills in healthy relationships. The first task of respect is gaining consent. In the case of communication, this means asking your partner if they're open to dialogue rather than just assuming they're ready to talk. The above phrases are examples of simple ways to communicate respect and set the tone for a positive conversation.

Focusing is another important skill for demonstrating respect in communication. If you find yourself easily distracted, take time to address any pressing needs before settling in for an important conversation. Close the door for privacy, turn down media noises, and let your partner know when you're ready to listen attentively.

Once your partner begins to share, work hard not to interrupt. If holding back your thoughts is difficult for you, focus on breathing deeply to soothe nerves, focus your mind, and listen well. Often, serial interrupters are worried that they won't be heard by their partner unless they interject. But interrupting has the opposite effect—it makes partners less likely to listen because they feel disrespected.

> TIP: If you find yourself lost when your partner is sharing something (it happens!), focus on the feelings rather than the details. Identify and reflect the feelings that you hear your partner expressing: "It sounds like you had a stressful day!" Summarizing your partner's stories by highlighting their feelings demonstrates care and respect.

HOLDING THE FLOOR

August and Ray weren't sure if their relationship could be saved—they both felt like their conversations circled around the same topics without progress.

"I try to tell Ray about how much I want to move—"

"August, our jobs are here!"

"And when I tell Ray, she doesn't seem to respond—"

"You never listen either, August."

August and Ray talked over each other, interrupting constantly and defensively. The therapist opened a side table drawer, pulled out a piece of tile flooring, and passed it to August. "You have the floor," the therapist commented, indicating that it was August's turn to talk. "Pass it to Ray when you're ready to listen."

The therapist asked Ray to turn toward August and listen attentively, emphasizing that they would each have plenty of time to share. August took a deep breath and continued, "I want to move closer to family."

"What else? Tell us more," the therapist encouraged.

"It's too expensive to live in Los Angeles, and we might have kids and need family support." August glanced tensely at Ray, but relaxed a bit when she didn't interrupt.

The therapist waited a beat, giving August a chance to expand further. Instead, August wept.

"I don't think there's anything else. I've just been holding that in for a long time."

Ray reached out to August. "I didn't know you wanted this so badly, August."

Creating the structure necessary for focused listening is essential in relationship therapy. By pausing your reactionary thoughts to listen to your partner, you are creating a space where major disclosures and core feelings can emerge naturally.

Ray and August had many complex topics to discuss in relationship therapy, but it turned out that their relationship was extremely empathetic as long as they were given the opportunity (and, often, reminders) to listen intently. With practice, they both learned to slow down, take a breath, take turns, and focus on their partner's experience.

How to Speak So Your Partner Hears You

Responsible communication begins with you. The secret to responsible communication is remembering that you can influence how your partner perceives your words. "You never take out the trash" lands differently than "I'm feeling run down. Would you be willing to help me with the trash?"

Psychologist Thomas Gordon developed the well-known communication strategy of using "I" statements, which encourage expression of thoughts and feelings without attributing them to a partner. "I feel lonely" is a statement of personal responsibility—"I" am taking ownership of my feeling, and "I" am sharing it with my partner.

Claiming your thoughts and feelings as your own is a key step in relational happiness. Try incorporating "I" statements into your relationship vocabulary.

Focus on Clear Communication

Specific and direct communication is key to keeping your relationship free from unnecessary anxiety. "We need to talk" may sound ominous to some couples because it's vague and abstract. But by clearly communicating your feelings and needs, you can relieve the burden of interpretation. Make it easier for your partner to impress you with their ability to meet your needs by taking a moment to plan the message that you want them to hear. To do this, write down "I feel ____ and I want ____." Pithy, direct statements get straight to the point so that your partner doesn't have to guess what you're trying to say and can instead focus on your feelings and objectives. Clear expression on your part helps cultivate receptive listening from your loving partner.

Communicate with Your Body Language

Have you ever noticed when you're addressing a difficult or emotional topic with your partner that you avoid eye contact or pull yourself away to create distance? Sometimes people pull back from their partner as a defensive mechanism to help them feel safe in a vulnerable environment.

If you know that your partner cares about how they've intentionally or unintentionally hurt you and is willing to change to reduce further harm, consider using soft physical touch during painful conversations. By maintaining eye contact and soothing touch (such as holding hands), you're acknowledging that your relationship is safe and committed to working through challenges together.

Pay attention to how your body reacts when you're in a state of heightened emotion. Notice your breath—is it shallow and high in your chest, indicating anxiety? Are you holding tension in your jaw, shoulders, or fists, as if you are subconsciously primed to fight? Now take a few slow, deep breaths deep into your diaphragm to relax your body and prepare for constructive communication.

Body language, tone, and volume speak louder than words. Try to be consistent with your physical cues and verbal content. For example, if you ask your partner for affection but cross your arms, your partner may sense defensiveness and feel threatened. Conversely, if you open your arms and ask for a hug, the words and the gesture both send a clear message that you want to connect.

When couples make a decision to reach out to each other when they're in pain, it usually means they're ready to empathize with their partner's emotions and humbly collaborate.

Kelsey and Soren were feeling disconnected. "I feel like we have a daily grind with work and chores, and then we go to bed," Kelsey shared, dazed. "I miss our long conversations and laughs. I don't know where that fits into our lives right now—we don't have hours to kill like we did in our early 20s."

Their therapist suggested a change of posture: "Kelsey, would you mind lying down on the couch? Soren, would you be up for grabbing a pillow to place on your lap or next to you for Kelsey to rest on?"

Kelsey relaxed, kicking her feet up. "This is nice after a long day!"

"That's the idea," the therapist responded. "I want you to look up and tell Soren about something that surprised you today. Big or small, it doesn't matter."

Soren naturally cradled Kelsey's head as she began to share, "Well, I was surprised when the barista got my order wrong this morning and gave me the extra drink."

"Now, Soren," the therapist interjected, "I want you to find a question to ask about anything that Kelsey shares. Try to pick questions that help Kelsey focus on her feelings. Don't share your opinions or thoughts in this exercise, just focus on asking questions."

"Okay," Soren said, gazing down at Kelsey. "What do you like to drink these days?"

"I switched from coffee to tea because I haven't been sleeping well," Kelsey responded.

"Oh!" said Soren. "What's been keeping you awake?"

"I've been stressed about my sister," Kelsey shared. "She's not doing well."

After Soren prompted Kelsey to share for five minutes, the therapist had them switch positions. "This works for me," Soren chirped. "Feel free to give me a head massage while you think of your questions!"

Kelsey followed the same structure, prompting Soren to share about something that surprised him recently and then following up with thoughtful questions.

After five more minutes, the therapist had them both sit up. They were both noticeably relaxed.

For many couples, taking turns to speak and listen for 10 minutes, while in body positions that are conducive to vulnerable sharing, is a game changer. The content of these conversations will vary from light to heavy, but therapists consistently notice a shift toward connection when couples break out of their habitual communication styles into a slower, focused, physically connected moment of sharing.

TIP: When asking your partner questions, try not to overuse *why* questions, since they can sound unintentionally accusatory when asked repetitively. Instead, mix in questions that begin with *who, what, when, where,* and *how.*

Lead with Kindness

Humans have a tendency to become who other people expect them to be. When name-calling or hurtful labels happen during conflicts, a "self-fulfilling prophecy" may occur wherein the victim aligns their behaviors with how they are perceived. For example, if you call your partner a "bad listener," they may become a perpetually bad listener, using the logic "if I'm a bad listener, why try to listen?" Conversely, when you kindly let your partner know that you find them lovable and worthy of respect, they are inspired to live up to those titles. Encourage your partner's potential by reflecting their "best self" back to them. For example, "I notice how you often try to be considerate of my feelings, so I want to share with you how I am feeling."

Kindness also fosters honesty and disclosure. When you refrain from judgment and treat your partner as you would want to be treated, they may choose to open up to you and share vulnerable thoughts and feelings. Help your relationship reach new depths of understanding by cultivating a safe space through kind communication.

State the Obvious and Get Specific

For the past few years, my husband has left little notes in our bathroom for me to find when I wake up. "Thank you for making daily lunches for the boys," one said. "I like how you look in your red dress," said another. Those daily reminders are powerfully touching because they are specific: I know that my husband notices me, knows me well, and appreciates the details in the life we create together.

Consider telling your partner what feels obvious to you. "I love you," "I'm attracted to you," and "I appreciate you" are true statements in most relationships that often get communicated less frequently as time goes on. Good communicators state the obvious, but great communicators get specific.

Tell a Good Story

Therapists know that narratives are at the heart of change. What's the story that you tell yourself about your relationship with your partner? For example, my pastors frequently remind each other, "We can do hard things." This phrase reminds them of the hardships they've worked to overcome in their relationship, encouraging them to persevere in their current battles.

The first question I often ask in couples therapy is: "Tell me the story of how you two met." I know that if couples can recall the positive qualities that initially drew them together, we can draw out the strengths of that first story and use those as inspiration while we navigate more challenging chapters of the relationship.

Try to remember a successful challenge that you and your partner have worked through. What is the story of that success? What did you learn about yourselves and your relationship? Commit to reminding each other of that prior victory with a word or phrase.

"We were always perfect, we continue to be perfect, and we'll always be perfect" is not a movie that I would watch. If you've worked through something challenging together, credit the qualities or beliefs that helped your relationship overcome it. You're the author of the story about your relationship—make it a good one!

HEALING IS A CHOICE

Jose and Stephanie had a history of infidelity in their relationship, but they were intent on making it work. "We love each other and have been together for so many years," they told their therapist. "We can't give it all up now."

They had tried to forget the past transgression, but ultimately found that the memory kept creeping back in. "Ever since the affair, every movie, TV show, and book seems to involve cheating. We can't seem to get past it."

Jose and Stephanie desperately wanted to remove the triggers to their relational trauma, but instead they needed to rewrite their story. "The story you tell yourselves, pretending that the affair didn't happen, may be increasing your relationship anxiety," the therapist suggested. "It's not a true story, and you keep getting caught in that reality. What if you told the truth?"

"The truth?" asked Jose, confused.

"The truth is that you two know that you can't ever completely go back to the pre-affair relationship. But you can choose healing."

Stephanie nodded. "Healing is a choice. It's a hard choice, but we're here in therapy because we need healing."

Once Stephanie and Jose shifted from avoidance of the affair to acknowledgment of the affair, they opted to remind each other of their commitment when triggers, like infidelity storylines in movies, arose. After their session, the couple experimented with embracing their history rather than running from it. "Healing is a choice," Stephanie wrote to Jose in an anniversary card that they showed their therapist. "Our relationship fell apart when we neglected it. Let's remember that our renewed commitment to each other is because of our pain, not despite our pain."

Long-term relationships often hold epic stories of pain and renewal. When couples can name the transformations they've endured, challenging memories become sources for inspiration.

Communicate Expectations

There are two common reasons couples don't communicate expectations. First, couples feel guilty for having expectations, and, second, they're so entrenched in their expectations that they don't even realize they have them. Both reasons usually cause trouble.

Everybody has hopes, preferences, plans, and norms—these are generally what form expectations. Familiarities, such as the roles each of your parents played in your household when you were a child or the cultural gender norms that are normative for you, often form unspoken expectations.

Think through your expectations in the following scenarios:

- It's your birthday. If your partner said and did nothing, how would you feel? What are your expectations?

- A family car is broken. Who fixes it or takes it to the mechanic? Are there expectations that a particular person would respond to certain responsibilities or chores in your home?

- You make dinner for your partner. Is an acknowledgment of this act expected?

- You're not feeling well. If your partner doesn't care for you, is that accepted? If not, what are your expectations?

Once you become aware of your expectations for assistance with household tasks, special days, illnesses, and gifts or services provided, it's critical to communicate these to your partner. Let them know how you may feel if your expectations are met and if they are not met.

It's critical to note that expectations are not demands—your partner doesn't have to comply with your expectations. Asking them if they can meet your expectation simply gives your partner a chance to consent or decline. And no matter what their response is, you'll likely appreciate knowing ahead of time.

Communicate Insecurities

Everybody has insecurities that seem obvious to them, but these insecurities are often nearly invisible to others. Rather than assuming that your partner is aware of your insecurities, choose a comfortable moment to share the ways you have internalized past criticism, trauma, or rejection so that your partner can be sensitive to these topics. For example:

- Is there a body part, skill, mental health challenge, or learning difference that you are insecure about?

- Do you ever feel like you don't measure up to expectations? When?

- Do you ever feel rejected or unwanted? When?

- Have you experienced a physical, emotional, or sexual trauma that has impacted your sense of safety or confidence?

- Are there certain topics or environments that make you feel uncomfortable or anxious?

It may be difficult to trust your partner with your insecurities, and that's understandable—sharing vulnerable insecurities feels like a risk. But if you endure the temporary anxiety, you can help prevent future pain in your relationship and make it more secure.

Communicate Future Goals

Communication is a vehicle that gets you where you want to go in your relationship. It's imperative that you and your partner know whether you share similar or complementary long-term objectives, personally and relationally.

TOPICS FOR DISCUSSION

1. Identify your goals for your life at one year, five years, 10 years, 20 years, 50 years.
2. Discuss your interest in long-term living arrangements, including where you would like to live, whether home purchasing is an objective, and whom you would like to live with (i.e., whether you would live alone as a couple or share housing with family members or roommates).
3. Talk about your desire to have or refrain from having children.
4. Name future career plans, including potential schooling, moves, and associated risks.
5. Discuss plans for health including work-life balance, and physical, social, and emotional care.
6. Explore whether your relationship involves working toward shared goals or simply supporting each other's goals.
7. Discuss topics that would not otherwise be easily incorporated into conversation. For example, do you or your family members have physical or mental health issues that may impact long-term goals?

Conversations about long-term plans may require flexibility—plans can change, just like humans can change. But by initiating important topics with your partner, you'll set the tone for continued conversations as your relationship progresses and new opportunities or challenges emerge.

Avoid Miscommunication

Miscommunication in relationships typically results from assumptions and undercommunication. When people assume that their partner is on the same page and neglect to check in with their understanding, communication reliably breaks down.

Instead, take ownership of your expectations by acknowledging that your partner is not a mind reader and cannot anticipate your needs and wants. If you would like your partner to say, do, or give you something, it's up to you to ask instead of assuming that they're aware of what you want.

After you've communicated with your partner, it's helpful to check each other's understanding. For example, if your partner says, "Let's meet up for dinner later," you may confirm, "So we'll leave work at 5 pm and meet here at 5:30 to get to the restaurant downtown around 6 pm—is that what you're thinking?" Checking for understanding takes time and effort, but in my experience most relational conflicts are the result of miscommunication. Skip the stress and confirm it!

> TIP: One technological leap that helps reduce relational miscommunication is sharing calendars. Couples who share a family calendar, either on paper or on their smartphones, can easily reference these resources to confirm their partner's plans.

Communicate Trust

Your commitment to your partner indicates that you trust them to help you more than hurt you; in other words, your relationship is likely built on trust. When your partner shows care for your well-being in their words and actions, it's reasonable to give them the benefit of the doubt.

One of the best ways to build and solidify trust in a relationship is by asking questions, which suggests, "I trust that you will be honest with me."

Let's say that your partner doesn't show up on time for a scheduled date. Rather than immediately blaming them for their insensitivity, it may be reasonable to ask your partner what happened as a gesture of trust that they didn't intend to hurt you.

Another hallmark of trust in a relationship is reciprocity—the knowledge that your partner will give as much to you as you do to them. Healthy relationships balance both partners' needs over time. For example, one partner may care for a sick child so that the other can work, and the working partner might pick up dinner as a gesture of care.

When your partner does something considerate, name it! Expressing gratitude for your partner out loud encourages them to continue to take your feelings and needs into account and boosts your relationship's satisfaction.

Communicate About Privacy

Do you care if your partner shares details about your struggles with their family or your intimate moments with their friends? If you have preferences about privacy with your partner, be sure to let them know.

Healthy relationships sometimes include trusted confidants who help the couple work through challenges or support positive relational growth. Talk with your partner about which individuals or professionals you both feel comfortable sharing sensitive information about your relationship with. Whom do you both trust for objective support? Do you want to be notified or included if your partner seeks guidance from these individuals?

Finding the balance of a strong support network for your relationship while respecting privacy requires thoughtful communication. You may opt to include the next strategy to make sure you and your partner land on the privacy decisions that are best for your relationship:

Evaluate What's Working . . . and What's Not

"How can I love you well?" my husband would routinely ask on our Friday night dates. His thoughtful question always implied three things:

1. That love is an action, not just a feeling

2. That there was always room for improvement in our relationship

3. That he was prepared to make changes

Having a regular opportunity to share casual or significant relational requests helps prevent couples from building up resentments, stuffing down feelings, or waiting until a conflict to communicate your concerns. This routine evaluation can also be a chance to reflect on progress in your relationship and reinforce experiences when you felt particularly loved or cared for by your partner.

Every relationship has strengths and challenges, and every person is constantly developing. This means that relationships don't ever reach a static arrival point of satisfaction. But by regularly evaluating what areas are working and what areas need adjustment, you'll increases your chances of being satisfied more often.

> TIP: Newly committed couples sometimes face the temptation to idealize their relationship and refrain from making relational requests. Instead, challenge yourselves to identify three ways that your partner can "love you well" in the next month.

Couple Check-In

You and your partner are now skilled communicators! You know how to listen well, speak with intention, and communicate about essential topics for relational health. In the next chapter, you'll explore how to build on communication and remain closely connected. That's right, you'll be learning all about intimacy. From boundaries to exploration, monogamy to romance, it's all covered in chapter 5.

Closeness

Couples who share meaningful physical and emotional intimacy typically stay together longer and have healthier relationships. But fostering that intimacy takes time, trust, commitment, and vulnerability.

Intimacy and Sex

I've often referred to intimacy as the "secret ingredient" for committed couples who thrive in their relationship. An enjoyable physical and emotional connection helps relieve stress, balance out relational challenges, and motivate shared effort in the relationship.

It's important that you and your partner cultivate a practice of intimacy that works for both of you. This chapter isn't just about sex, but intimacy in general—the private, set-apart time that couples spend nurturing their physical and emotional bond—and I'll provide strategies for fostering a healthy connection with intimacy.

Trust

Trust is the foundation of connection for most couples. As each partner cares for their partner and honors their commitments, they know that they will receive care and consideration in return. Though the phrase "broken trust" may provoke anxiety, the reality is that trust is broken for most couples on a regular basis. Anytime partners don't fulfill their promises (even when it's a small promise, such as completion of a chore), trust is damaged. But when partners demonstrate thoughtful action and sacrifice, trust is built.

Pick out the three important ways that your partner can demonstrate trustworthiness in your relationship and have your partner do the same.

I trust you when you …

1. Follow through with your commitments—when you say what you mean and mean what you say

2. Avoid situations that could be destructive for our relationship (such as unfaithfulness, addiction, etc.)

3. Treat me with dignity and honor my boundaries

4. Express feelings in a productive, rather than destructive, way

5. Are willing to sacrifice for the sake of our relationship

6. Budget your time so that you can complete tasks or help

7. Are consistent and reliable

8. Prioritize honesty, telling the truth even when it's hard

9. Are open with your thoughts and feelings

10. Demonstrate care, kindness, and respect for me

11. Treat other people well

12. Make intentional choices according to your value system

13. Confess mistakes

14. Ask for help

15. Discuss issues and look for solutions to problems

Setting Expectations

In order to feel pleasure and connection, we usually need to feel safe and secure, and one of the best ways to build that security is to set clear expectations.

Discuss with your partner whether you believe the following statements are true or false regarding your relationship:

1. We may have different preferences for connection. For example, one of us may have higher desire for physical or emotional connection than the other.

2. Our relationship requires work in order to grow, including our physical and emotional relationship.

3. Since we can't read each other's minds, communicating our desires is important.

4. We will honor mutual consent above either individual's desire in our relationship. For example, acts of physical intimacy will not proceed unless both of us are comfortable.

Once you and your partner have defined expectations in your relationship, you may feel more confident to communicate your feelings, thoughts, and desires.

Communication

My sex therapy professor in graduate school used to joke, "If a couple comes to you saying that they're having issues with communication, they're really having issues with sex. And if a couple comes to you saying that they're having issues with sex, they're really having issues with communication."

This humorous reflection has proven true in my years in relationship therapy. Couples who thrive in their physical connection tend to communicate frequently and specifically about their feelings, thoughts, and desires.

To explore how communication can improve physical connection with your partner, try this exercise:

Turn on some relaxing music, dim the lights, and invite your partner to receive a hand, head, back, or neck massage from you. Massaging a non-sexual organ takes the pressure off performance and allows you both to focus on positive communication. At another time, the communication skills learned through this exercise may be transferred to overtly sexual touch.

Ask your partner which body part they would like you to focus on. Encourage them to consistently communicate with words, gestures, or positive sounds while guiding your touch. If your partner wants more of a particular action, invite them to ask for more and to describe the degree of pressure and pace that will make it more pleasurable.

Try to avoid negative language, if possible. For example, if your partner is displeased with the massage, instead of them saying, "Don't do that!," suggest that they ask you to do something more desirable. If they are enjoying the massage, they could say, "Keep massaging that spot," or, "I like that amount of pressure," rather than, "Don't move."

After focusing on massaging your partner for approximately 10 minutes, switch. Have your partner massage you while you guide their actions.

How much you enjoy these massages will depend on how well you communicate with each other. Try repeating the exercise daily until you both feel as though you are giving and receiving an ideal massage.

TAKING THE PRESSURE OFF

Casey and Suzuki were in their therapist's office discussing a sexual drought. After a series of health issues and work issues, their sexual intimacy had gradually decreased until sexual contact stopped altogether.

The feelings of shame and embarrassment about their predicament were equaled by the feelings of anxiety and awkwardness that they now felt about physical intimacy with each other. As a result, when they did try to engage in physical affection, they found it difficult to achieve the bodily responses they hoped for.

As a result of these challenges, both Casey and Suzuki retreated from physical affection in various ways: Casey turned to pornography, and Suzuki became numb and withdrawn from sexuality, wondering if perhaps they were asexual.

The therapist suggested that Casey and Suzuki both prioritize relaxation and decrease pressure on sexual intercourse.

"What helps you feel attractive and confident?" the therapist asked, curious.

"When I wear a dress and lipstick, I feel like I'm myself again," Suzuki shared.

"When I'm able to help Suzuki enjoy herself, that's what helps me feel capable," Casey reflected.

The therapist suggested that Casey plan a date where Suzuki would dress up, and they would come home early to light some candles and snuggle. Suzuki would communicate her preferences for physical touch, guiding Casey in either sexual or non-sexual touch—whatever she wanted. The objective? Enjoyment, confidence, and relaxation.

The next week, Suzuki and Casey sat closer on the couch. They described a relaxing and physically intimate date, with another one planned for the weekend.

A couple's beliefs about physical affection sometimes matter more than the specific acts themselves. When couples feel connected, cared for, and confident, they feel free to explore their physical relationship and often naturally develop a number of ways to connect with their partner emotionally and sexually.

Set Aside Time

In my therapy practice, I've learned that a feeling of disconnection is the most common concern of many couples. So when couples want to rekindle their romance, the first step has to be setting aside time.

Going to bed at the same time, spending quality time together during the day before exhaustion has set in, lingering together before heading to work, and going on vacations together are all ways couples can give their relationship the time it needs to foster connection.

Take time with your partner now and identify five meaningful moments of romantic connection that you've shared together, such as a treasured date, trip, or experience. Try to include examples of memories that have included planning as well as examples of memories that are unplanned and spontaneous.

Discuss the elements that laid the foundation for intimate or romantic moments in these memories.

- Did the fact that you had plenty of time help you and your partner foster connection?

- Did you set your responsibilities aside?

- Were you well rested?

- Were there other elements of romance, such as a shared meal or a thoughtful gesture, that helped set the scene?

Understanding that rushed lives often lead to disconnection and that leisure time can bring intimacy is important. When couples realize that their disconnection is related to a busy lifestyle laden with responsibilities, they often feel motivated to make room for their relationship to come up for air.

Prioritize Dates

When my husband and I started dating, I enrolled in a series of courses about the psychology of successful relationships. The renowned professors (Drs. Les and Leslie Parrott) emphasized the importance of weekly dates, making such an impression that my husband and I have gone on weekly dates for the past 19 years.

I have found that it's easiest for couples to begin a practice of routine date nights early in their commitment. While couples at this early stage may be naturally inclined to spend time together anyway, getting into the routine of date nights allows them to continue the practice more easily when life gets busy and their motivation wanes.

QUESTION FOR DISCUSSION

Discuss whether you and your partner would like to include a weekly date night in your routine. If so, commit to a day to ensure it remains a priority.

Several studies indicate that couples derive the most benefits from novel dates, so consider skipping your weekly pizza joint or show for date night. The rush of learning something new, jumping around at the local trampoline park, or taking a thrilling amusement park ride may build a neuropsychological association to the excitement of spending time with your partner.

Take some time to explore novel date ideas, using the first three ideas to begin the brainstorming process. Try to include some remote date options (for example: my husband and I recently went on a virtual chocolate factory tour, complete with a tasting of shipped chocolate bars) as well as some at-home options (after all, "sex starts in the kitchen"!) to add some variety and flexibility to your date night routine.

1. Learn a new skill, such as attending a cooking, dance, or painting class

2. Play a sport or spend time outdoors

3. Attend a concert or a play

4. _____

5. _____

6. _____

Connect Emotionally

Emotional intimacy often spurs physical intimacy. When couples enhance their relationship with sensitive questions, thoughtful reflections, and encouraging words, it helps release tension and cultivate affection that leads to intimacy.

To further build emotional connection with your partner, answer the following questions and share your results:

1. I feel most connected when you ...

    a. Ask me about my feelings or experiences
    b. Remember things I have shared
    c. Vulnerably open up to me
    d. Demonstrate trustworthiness
    e. _____

2. I feel most supported when you ...

    a. Validate my feelings
    b. Help me
    c. Take responsibility for tasks without being asked
    d. Speak encouraging words to me
    e. _____

3. It feels safe to be vulnerable with you when ...

    a. We have time together
    b. You initiate connection
    c. We work through challenges together
    d. I feel accepted by you
    e. _____

Play Around Together

Play—the ability to be silly, creative, and unrestrained with your partner—is a wonderful antidote to the pressures of daily life and often a welcome form of intimacy in romantic relationships. It's also a highway to pleasure and connection, enjoying the journey without worrying about the destination.

Research indicates that playful couples enjoy high satisfaction with their relationship, greater feelings of intimacy, and productive communication. But what if you and your partner consider yourselves serious introverts? The good news is that playfulness isn't dependent on personality so much as it's a skill to be honed. If you and your partner are bookworms, look for puns or create a secret language. Explore childlike games in the privacy of your home, or take on the roles of characters from a favorite book or show. Play provides relationships the freedom to be goofy without judgment, joining each other in unbridled vulnerability and joy.

Before couples can feel comfortable engaging in playful connection though humor or physical touch, they need to establish safety by resolving conflicts and respecting boundaries.

According to psychotherapist Esther Perel, "You cannot play, take risks, or be creative when you don't have a minimum of safety, because you need a level of unselfconsciousness to be able to experience excitement and pleasure." Once couples have established trustworthy relationships, they are free to play, unencumbered by guilt, shame, or stress.

QUESTIONS FOR DISCUSSION

1. Are there any barriers to playfulness in our relationship?
2. Tell me about the last time you remember laughing or expressing creativity. What was the context?
3. What helps you feel alive? What helps you feel free?

> TIP: Sometimes couples feel awkward during physical intimacy, even when they trust each other deeply. When in doubt, play! Laughter and play can relieve anxiety while paving the way for physical affection.

Open to Explore

Now that you and your partner are a committed couple, you may feel free to begin to let down guards and explore various forms of connection. It's important for exploration to feel fun, without adding undue expectation or pressure.

An essential step toward authentic intimacy is knowing yourself. Take some time to write down personal fantasies: the particular dreams that encapsulate your preferences, needs, and desires. Imagine if you felt totally and completely known, loved, respected, free, happy, or fulfilled. What would be the context surrounding those experiences?

Once you have a strong sense of your own desires, you can consider sharing them with your partner in your own timing. Though communicating vulnerable personal fantasies can sometimes feel uncomfortable, your best chance at getting your desires met is by sharing these hopes within a trustworthy relationship.

> TIP: Some couples find it helpful to create a menu for desirable physical affection. Write a menu of physically affectionate behaviors for your partner to try if it's within their comfort zone.

Boundaries

"Boundaries help us keep the good in and the bad out," wrote author Henry Cloud. By setting boundaries in your relationship, you'll each take responsibility for your own choices and create a foundation of trust upon which you can build authentic intimacy.

Though it may be tempting for committed couples to reject the idea of boundaries with each other, the truth is all relationships include expectations, and expectations are examples of boundaries. For example, if you expect your partner to be monogamous, you are setting a boundary around a faithful relationship.

Boundaries for emotional and physical intimacy in a romantic relationship are often progressive, providing opportunities for deeper connection as time goes on and commitments to the relationship increase. If you set limits with your partner and they respond with care, you can change your boundary as you feel comfortable.

Define your current boundaries with your partner regarding:

1. Monogamy: Do you expect exclusive commitment in your relationship? Discuss expectations for both external relationships and pornography.

2. Physical intimacy: How should consent for physical affection be communicated?

3. Contraception: What forms of contraception will you use, if engaging in intercourse?

4. Triggers: What acts of affection are currently off-limits due to negative experiences, anxiety, moral convictions, or discomfort?

5. Breaches of trust: How do you plan to communicate to your partner if you are considering breaking your relationship's commitment? Or if you feel that they crossed a boundary? Are there opportunities to evaluate the status of trust in the relationship outside of a crisis?

When couples engage in the hard work of identifying their personal boundaries, expressing them to their partner, and keeping them, trust builds and intimacy flourishes.

RETURNING TO THE PRESENT MOMENT

Emma had been sexually harassed by a family friend as a child. She coped with the sexualized comments about her body by becoming sexually promiscuous in high school and beyond, with no regard for her safety or emotional well-being. Emma's family hadn't intervened when she drew their attention to the inappropriate behavior of the family friend, teaching Emma that her feelings and needs were irrelevant—in other words, boundaries didn't matter.

In her 30s, Emma settled down with a loving partner, but she came to the therapy office because she felt depressed about their relationship. "On paper, this is my dream spouse," Emma said, tearfully. "So why don't I feel excited about our relationship?"

After a few sessions, it became apparent that Emma was feeling dissociated and numb. Rather than disliking her relationship with her partner, Emma didn't feel anything at all.

"When have you felt this way before?" the therapist asked.

After some time, Emma chose to disclose her history of trauma, indicating that she cut herself off from her feelings so as not to absorb the pain of her reality. Dissociating from pain had helped Emma survive when she was younger, but her body hadn't gotten the message that she was now safe.

Emma and her therapist discussed a variety of options for treating her trauma, but one of Emma's favorite new coping tools included grounding. Grounding is a technique that acknowledges that anxiety fixates your attention on the past trauma and projects that experience onto a present moment like a recurring nightmare. To compensate for this, grounding encourages focusing on the present moment by using the five senses: sound, touch, smell, taste, and sight. When Emma became triggered by fears of unsafety, even when her partner was considerate and respectful of her boundaries, she gently found opportunities to focus on her senses in the present moment, often keeping her favorite music, perfume, foods, and pictures nearby. By inviting herself back to the present, she often felt secure. As a result of Emma's anxiety reduction, she was able to focus less on survival and more on tuning in to her feelings and desires.

Take Risks

Emotional and physical growth in committed relationships often requires you to take small steps outside your comfort zone. If you and your partner have a long track record of trust, respect, and honored boundaries, challenge yourselves to risk more vulnerability to enhance your connection.

When couples allow themselves to be physically or emotionally vulnerable, they give their fears the chance to dissipate. For example, if a person felt self-conscious about their body and risked leaving the light on during physical intimacy, they may find their partner attracted to their physical form, diminishing the insecurities that act as a barrier to physical affection.

Risk-taking is the cost of progress when it comes to intimacy. Take time to consider risks such as disclosing unspoken desires, fears, secrets, insecurities, and joys. Consider asking your partner to experiment with new activities or forms of intimacy. Risking vulnerability may feel scary, but trustworthy relationships are generally free from ridicule or insensitive rejection.

What risks are you ready to take?

Express Gratitude

Life can be difficult, and recognition helps create resilience. When you say "thank you" for specific sacrifices and efforts that benefit the relationship, you are cultivating a sense of connection and respect with your partner. Couples often feel seen and appreciated when they give each other regular low-key affirmations. A quick "thanks for getting the groceries" or "thanks for working so hard for our family" costs nothing and means everything.

What are three things that you're each thankful for in your relationship?

1. _____

2. _____

3. _____

Expressing specific affirmations and gratitude says, "I am intricately involved in your life and I don't take you for granted. I respect your time, and I want you to know that your efforts are valued." Unless your partner communicates otherwise, it's likely safe to assume that regular expressions of gratitude will build an even tighter bond between you.

Prioritize Joy Over Performance and Comparison

The purpose of vulnerable intimacy is to build enjoyable connection with your partner. Blissful union comes from the experience of being fully known and fully loved. Unfortunately, the vulnerability of physical and emotional intimacy can also promote feelings of insecurity.

If you've ever felt anxious that you are not living up to your partner's expectations, afraid that you're experiencing a less fulfilling relationship than others, or dwelling on feelings of shame, it may be helpful to work through anxiety with a mental health professional and refocus on the joys of intimacy in your relationship with your partner.

When you focus on performing in your relationship, intimate moments can feel like working toward a goal or evaluation. But when you focus on enjoyment, you can more easily return to the present moment, where anxieties dissipate. By prioritizing joy, couples can take breaks from focusing on past pain or future worries and intentionally draw their attention to feelings of gratitude for their current relationship. Pause to ask yourself, "What am I thankful for *right now* in my relationship with my partner?" Awareness is the most efficient path to joy in most relationships.

Have you ever heard the phrase, "Comparison is the thief of joy"? Because of the prevalence of pornography and the heavily edited or manufactured appearances of celebrities and influencers in the media, many couples compare their bodies or sexual relationship to unrealistic sexualized images. Refocusing on the comfort and enjoyment of your relationship requires a release of judgment—embracing your connection with your partner as fully your own and viewing other experiences outside your relationship as irrelevant.

THE GHOSTS OF EXES PAST

"I can't stop thinking about his exes. I follow them on social media, worrying that they made Blake happier than I do."

Hayden was distraught with anxiety and felt tortured by obsessive thoughts. Each time she felt anxious about being "enough," compulsion kicked in and she found herself constantly trying to please Blake and evaluate his response. This anxiety pattern impacted every facet of their relationship, including physical affection.

"I feel like the harder I try, the more insecure I feel," Hayden reflected, frustrated.

Hayden's behaviors were in response to a belief that fear was necessary. Anxiety led her to believe that Blake's affections could turn at any moment and that maintaining Blake's constant satisfaction was necessary for their relationship to continue. So Hayden took control and attempted to manage Blake's satisfaction—yet her anxiety continued.

Ultimately, Hayden needed to believe that she was worthy of love and that even if the relationship with Blake ended, her life would continue with meaning and purpose. As Hayden worked in therapy to address past pains that led to her development of insecurity, she was able to accept that she'd taken painful rejections from past relationships personally. "I'm ready to have my ex stop defining me! I know who I am, and my ex's choice to end our relationship doesn't determine who I am."

Because Hayden was finally ready to accept that she was lovable, she made a choice to act accordingly. Seeking mutually enjoyable activities and communicating her own feelings and preferences became the norm. To Hayden's delight, Blake seemed even more attracted to her now that she felt confident and self-assured.

Consider Your Self-Worth

1. Do your feelings of insecurity or lack of self-worth ever get in the way of connecting with your partner?

2. If so, where did those feelings develop?

3. What helps you believe that you are worthy of love?

Altruism Is an Aphrodisiac

One of the most surprising secrets to a healthy connection with your partner may be building relationships with other people. When couples jointly care for their relationships with children, family members, friends, and community members, they often feel more connected to each other.

You and your partner are likely attracted to good character, so when you both act like good parents, children, siblings, neighbors, and citizens, you're ultimately building intimacy in your relationship.

Similarly, kindness and respect in your relationship with your partner foster desire that lasts. In therapy, people often reflect that they are most attracted to their partner's care and regard for them. So if you see a task that could help your partner, do it! If you have a compliment to share, say it! Thoughtful gestures and admiring words are often the glue that holds relationships together.

QUESTIONS FOR DISCUSSION

Reflect on these questions with your partner to share ideas about how to build kindness and respect into your relationship.

1. When have you felt most respected by your partner?
2. What kind gesture or words from your partner have stuck with you?
3. Who are the people that you and your partner can care for together, outside of yourselves?

When two people are mutually focused on building up each other, and the community around them, the relationship often becomes a source of joy. Let your relationship become a force for good and, in return, reap the benefits that come with increased desire and satisfaction with your partner.

Couple Check-In

You and your partner have bravely explored your emotional and physical feelings, thoughts, and desires, laying the groundwork for meaningful intimacy. By learning about communication, expectations, boundaries, methods for building emotional and physical intimacy, and common barriers to closeness, you are now equipped with essential skills for connection.

In the next chapter, we'll tackle conflict resolution and how to regulate your emotions and solve problems in your relationship.

CHAPTER 6

Conflict

Conflict is to be expected in long-term relationships, and this chapter will help you and your partner navigate it productively. Learn how to fight well, and your relationship will improve with each challenge you work through together.

Navigating Conflict Constructively

Conflict plays an important role in committed relationships. It helps define expectations, promote change, and ensure the relationship meets both people's needs. Couples who argue and resolve conflicts effectively are demonstrating that they are invested in the relationship and care about its growth. In fact, partners who argue toward productive outcomes have a much higher chance of enjoying a happy relationship.

So what does it mean to fight well? In this chapter, you'll develop a plethora of conflict resolution strategies designed to help you thrive in your relationship with your partner.

Ready, set, fight!

No Judgment Here

One of the most important characteristics of a good learner is to be nonjudgmental and focused on discerning what's true above all else. As we explore the nuances of how you and your partner engage in conflict, I encourage you to take this nonjudgmental position, determining what is helpful and hurtful in your approach to conflict resolution without letting feelings like shame get in the way of productive learning.

The truth is, couples who "never fight" aren't perfect and couples who "always fight" aren't necessarily failing. If you can get curious about why you fight, you and your partner will ultimately identify your underlying needs and put yourselves on a fast track to satisfying conflict resolution.

Content Versus Feelings

When individuals and couples in my therapy office share about conflicts with their partners, they tend to focus on the content of the conflict—what happened and what was said. One of the strategies I use to help couples get to the core of their conflicts is to shift away from content and instead focus on feelings. The content of the argument rarely matters after the heat of the conflict wears off, but the feelings represent pain that may recur on a daily basis, sometimes for the entirety of a person's life. If I can help my clients identify their cycles of pain, the vulnerable feelings that represent their greatest fears and insecurities, then I can begin to equip them with the techniques that will help them take control of their emotional responses.

Neuropsychological research indicates that humans develop neural pathways—thought highways that replay certain messages again and again—primarily during childhood and in emotionally powerful circumstances. For example, when a child hears a critique from an older sibling or a parent, they may form a neural pathway that repeats, "You're not good enough." When that individual grows up and engages in a tense moment with a partner, that neural pathway saying, "You're not good enough," may flare up again.

Learning what messages your brain plays on autopilot due to past pains can become your superpower. If you know your insecurities and weaknesses, you'll soon become adept at responding to your fears and regulating your own emotions without requiring your partner to perfectly tend to your emotions for you.

To recognize your pain patterns, make good use of your body's natural defense mechanisms. Complete the following exercise to read your body's cues for deep-rooted psychological pain:

1. In the next week, take notice when your breathing is strained, your cheeks are flushed, or your heart is pounding.

2. Determine whether or not you are in a physical crisis. If your safety is not at risk and your physiological reaction is stronger than necessary for a given event, you have likely discovered a subconscious insecurity.

3. Decipher the story you are telling yourself about the triggering event. For example, you may believe that you are out of control, disrespected, powerless, or devalued.

4. Repeat this exercise to find repetition. Did you identify the same storyline more than once? If so, you may have discovered the emotional neural pathways that trigger conflicts with your partner. The storyline that causes you the most distress is your pain pattern.

By becoming an expert on the routine insecurities that your brain replays during conflict, you can address the root of the issue rather than feel caught in an endless cycle of repetitive conflicts. Communicating your pain points without blaming your partner allows them to connect and empathize with you when you need it most. But that doesn't mean you'll be asking your partner to become a caretaker for your emotions—the following sections will outline ways to take ownership of your emotions and regulate them.

Pull Back from Conflict to Emotionally and Physically Regulate

There are times when it's better not to communicate with your partner. When it comes to communication, it's very important to pick your moment to reduce the potential for further conflict. Consider tending to physical needs before communicating at length with your spouse. If you are:

1. Hungry

2. Tired

3. Overstimulated (for example, your senses are on overload and you feel stressed)

Eating, getting rest, and relaxing in a soothing environment is the responsible thing to do when you're preparing for a conversation with your partner.

Just as it wouldn't be prudent to start a conversation with your partner while hangry, it also isn't wise to engage in dialogue when your heart is racing. Difficult emotions such as anger often trigger a physiological reaction that impacts brain function. When the body goes into a fight-or-flight response during a conflict, blood flow is reduced to the prefrontal cortex and you're less able to clearly communicate or anticipate the consequences of the conflict.

If you notice a feeling that psychologists describe as "flooding," in which emotions feel overwhelming and your body is under stress (usually indicated by a heart rate over 100 beats per minute), take a break to soothe yourself before communicating with your partner. Perhaps a walk in nature or a relaxing shower would be a calming environment where you can practice the following emotion-regulation technique.

Regulate Your Emotions
Using The Four Steps

The communication technique that I use more often than anything else in my therapy practice is the Four Steps. It's an emotion-regulation technique created by psychologist Terry Hargrave and Sharon Hargrave, LMFT, which is designed to help individuals understand where their pain is rooted and ground themselves in the reality of the present. The Four Steps can be used to emotionally prepare yourself for communication with your partner, or they can be used in direct communication with your partner.

STEP 1: SAY HOW YOU FEEL

Do you ever feel like you have the same conflicts with your partner again and again? It's likely that you're experiencing sensitivity to a particularly painful emotion. The first step of emotional regulation is to identify what you are feeling when you are in pain, boldly naming your emotion in its rawest form. Using the most vulnerable language possible, confront the emotion head-on by naming precisely how you feel.

For example, rather than saying, "I feel frustrated." or, "I feel upset," try picking a more specific, vulnerable word instead. Typically, our most intense emotions are rooted in a desire to feel loved and safe. In contrast, when people are in pain, they may perceive themselves as unloved or unsafe. These emotions might be more specifically felt as being *unworthy, hopeless, unwanted, unappreciated, insignificant, alone, disrespected, powerless, inadequate, unknown, out of control, defective, unable to measure up to expectations,* or *devalued.*

Emotional awareness can be challenging, and identifying the feelings of pain underneath stress or frustration may leave you feeling drained. Fortunately, our emotional lives tend to be cyclical. What does this mean? When you pinpoint a particular feeling of pain, there's a good chance that this feeling is a constant in your life. If you can work to understand the roots of that feeling, you may be more equipped to respond to that emotion when it cycles back.

QUESTION FOR REFLECTION

Once you have identified one or more of your feeling words, reflect on when you first remember feeling that way. What is the origin of this emotion? Perhaps when you were in a more helpless or less resilient time in your life, you felt this particular pain—and the feeling stuck.

> TIP: The origin stories of our pain can be processed in counseling sessions, through journaling, or in dialogue with your partner. Make a plan for addressing the origin of your typical feelings of pain. You didn't just wake up one day and decide, "You know, I'd like to feel inadequate!" Practice self-compassion by tenderly acknowledging your pain's origin story in a secure environment.

STEP 2: CALL YOURSELF OUT

Once you identify your primary feeling of pain, you have begun the process of taking responsibility for your feelings. The next step is to take that further by naming the destructive coping mechanisms that you typically react with when you are in pain during conflicts with your partner. The four most common destructive coping mechanisms result from the instinct for fight-or-flight reactions:

- Blame others (it's your fault I'm in pain)

- Shame self (it's my fault I'm in pain)

- Take control (of others or situations in an attempt to create a sense of safety)

- Withdraw (escape)

By acknowledging tendencies for one or more of these destructive coping mechanisms, you'll be less likely to habitually, mindlessly engage in these patterns. For example, saying, "I'm feeling unloved and I'm tempted to blame you," offers you a chance to evaluate that feeling and decision before acting on autopilot.

Where did you learn your destructive coping mechanism? You may find that you mimic the patterns of your parents. Or that you opt for coping mechanisms that are reactive to the destructive coping mechanisms your parents modeled (e.g., someone with a controlling parent might be tempted to withdraw).

What are the consequences of your destructive coping mechanisms? How do these habits hurt you or your partner?

STEP 3: NAME WHAT'S TRUE

Feelings are often logical based on a person's life experiences. For instance, it makes sense that an individual might feel unheard if they had a self-absorbed parent. Because humans tend to compile our emotional experiences over our lifetimes, we are prone to projecting past feelings onto current life experiences with a partner.

The process of emotional regulation is an extension of mindfulness—the practice of grounding oneself in the present moment. When you experience a particularly sensitive feeling of pain, you may subconsciously be reminded of the other times you had that same feeling of pain, thus intensifying your emotional experience. In this case, you may be dealing with not simply the present emotional trigger, but also the cumulative emotional triggers from your past.

So what can you do to ground yourself when you experience distressing emotions in your relationship? You can name what is true, in this moment, about your identity, your relationship, and your choices.

Some examples of a "truth statement" in the emotional regulation process might look like this:

"I feel inadequate, and I'm tempted to shame myself. *But the truth is I'm bringing valuable skills into our relationship,* so I'll choose to work hard at what I can control, without shame."

"I feel devalued, and I'm tempted to withdraw. *But the truth is I'm loved by my partner,* so I'll try to stay engaged and communicate my needs."

When you consider your particular feelings of pain, are they telling the whole truth or a partial truth? It's important to try to create a truth statement that "widens the lens" to tell the whole story, since pain often fixates on particularly difficult situations. For example, if you feel unheard in a conflict with your partner, though they typically listen well, challenge yourself to name the "bigger truth" that "though I am not being heard in this current conflict, I know that you typically listen well."

STEP 4: RESPOND, DON'T REACT

The last step of communicating with regulated emotions is making an intentional choice to act based on what you believe is true about yourself, your relationship, or your options. For example, if you identify that you feel (Step 1) dismissed and are able to call yourself out (Step 2) for being tempted to withdraw, but recognize that the truth is (Step 3) that your partner doesn't hear you because you haven't been clearly asserting your needs, you might intentionally decide (Step 4) to clearly communicate your feelings and thoughts.

Couples who take time when they are emotionally overwhelmed to identify their particular feelings of pain and explore whether their emotions are accurately depicting the current circumstances in their relationship have much more efficient conflicts.

Have you ever felt trapped in a conflict while you and your partner engage in intense arguing or the silent treatment? When couples are in a reactive mode, they tend to impulsively act out their feelings on repeat until they're exhausted. But when couples slow down, take a breather, and thoughtfully examine their feelings, they find conflicts resolve much more quickly. Problem-solving tends to come relatively easily when both partners are responsible and emotionally regulated.

BREAKING THE CYCLE

Oscar and Casey were used to drawn-out conflicts that lasted days without resolution, and it became worse after Oscar recently lost his job.

In the course of therapy, Oscar had already determined that feeling unloved and not good enough were frequent experiences in his life, even before his job loss. To cope with feeling unloved, Oscar often defensively blamed Casey in the midst of their conflicts.

Casey's emotional patterns were a little different from Oscar's. Rather than struggling with feelings of being unloved, Casey often felt out of control. To cope with these feelings, Casey often became anxious and controlling in the relationship—and the anxiety was only getting worse during Oscar's unemployment.

Oscar and Casey were stuck in a vicious cycle, in which their feelings of pain triggered further emotional pain in their partner:

Oscar feels not good enough ⟶ *blames Casey* ⟶ *Casey feels out of control* ⟶ *controls Oscar* ⟶ *Oscar feels not good enough*

To break through this cycle, Oscar was encouraged to "ground" his feelings of being unloved by determining what he truly believed about love, apart from his feelings.

"I know that Casey loves me, even though I don't often feel it when we're fighting," Oscar began. "I also know that I'm lovable, and I know that even when I mess up, I am loved by God."

"Thank you, Oscar," affirmed their therapist. "What would you do if you knew for sure that you were loved by Casey and lovable and beloved by God? Would you still find yourself blaming Casey?"

"I think I would feel pretty confident, actually. There would still be problems to solve since I need to find a job, but I don't think I would need to blame Casey in the process."

"That's great, Oscar," reflected their therapist. "Now I want you to say all of that together—what you're feeling, how you reactively cope with those feelings, what you know is true, and how you'll choose to respond to that reality."

"Okay," Oscar said. "I often feel like I'm not good enough, and I'm tempted to blame you, Casey, for that. But the truth is you love me despite my flaws, and I know that I'm lovable and bring a lot to our relationship. God also loves me just as I am. So I'm going to choose to practice confidence as I problem-solve instead of letting insecurities take hold."

The beauty of Oscar regulating his emotions was that it completely redirected the conflict with Casey. Since Oscar was no longer reactive, defenses came down and feelings softened for both partners.

With respect for Oscar, Casey was able to make a similar commitment. "I'm prone to feeling unsafe and out of control," Casey began. "And to deal with that feeling, I often try to take control and give in to anxiety. But I know that you are trustworthy to work through these job challenges together, and I know that I am resourceful in the face of difficult circumstances. So I'll choose to relax, because I am safer than I feel."

By taking a few minutes to regulate their emotions before attempting to brainstorm ideas to address Oscar's job loss, Oscar and Casey saved themselves from days of harmful conflict. Because they shifted their attitude before the discussion began, they could remain open and connected in the midst of a typically hot topic.

Curate Your Communication

Emotions tend to pile on top of one another—one painful experience reminds you of other similarly painful memories, resulting in an urge to address all of the pain at once. For example:

"You *always* ignore me! You *never* pay attention to me!"

The issue, in these cases, is a massive emotional need: The individual feels unloved and needs to feel cherished. Valid as this may be, the issue is simply too big to be addressed by a therapist in a single session, much less by a partner outside of therapy. In order to have a successful dialogue that meets emotional needs and helps necessary change occur, the hurting individual needs to edit down their objective by focusing on a single incident, feeling, or need. For example:

"Last night at the party, I felt like you paid more attention to our friend than me. I felt ignored and insecure, but I think if we can connect tonight, I'll feel much better."

This is beneficial in two ways. It sets up the hurting individual for care by clearly and directly stating their feelings and needs, and it sets up the partner for success by identifying a way they can practically address the painful feelings. Remember that clear, specific communication is more vulnerable than indirect anger or distance, but relational growth is well worth the effort.

INTENTION VERSUS IMPACT

"You mocked me!" Jack seethed.

"I was just making a joke to cut the silence. You were ignoring me," retorted Olivia.

"I was trying to focus on work so that we could pay the bills," Jack replied curtly.

Their therapist cut in. "Look, it may be tempting to argue about the facts of what happened, but *perception* matters far more. You two may be ready to give me the play-by-play of your argument, in hopes that I will play referee. But I want to know what you are feeling."

The therapist knew that if they indulged Jack and Olivia in giving the rundown of events, the couple would leave the office angrier after ruminating on their disagreement. Empathy comes from humbly trying to see a situation from a partner's perspective, so their therapist decided to lead them in that direction.

"Focus on what your partner feels and try to understand the intention behind their actions."

After sharing and listening during the session, Olivia learned that though her intention was to connect with Jack, the impact was that he felt demeaned. Jack learned that though his intention was to focus on important work tasks, the impact was that Olivia felt dismissed.

By purposefully separating intent from impact, their empathy for their partner had room to grow. Olivia and Jack both learned to communicate their initial intentions while humbly acknowledging that their actions had unintended consequences. Rather than battling for the title of Who's Right, Olivia affirmed Jack's sacrifices and responsibilities with work, while Jack expressed gratitude for Olivia's attempts at connection in the midst of their busy lives.

Problem-Solve with Creativity

"Let's go grab some takeout."

"No, I want to go to a restaurant."

Have you ever found yourself at an impasse when trying to make a simple decision with your partner? If you are both emotionally regulated and yet still cannot agree on how to solve a problem, challenge yourselves with creative problem-solving.

Begin by writing down as many solutions as you possibly can—the more, the better. Expand your problem-solving by considering the underlying needs. With the food example above, is the problem hunger? Or is it deeper—for instance, a yearning for a particular environment, a sense of being cared for, or perhaps a need for relaxation? List more ideas that tend to the identified underlying needs.

The brainstorming process helps couples learn to identify multiple solutions, often providing opportunities for mutually agreeable options. When you feel competitive, get creative!

> TIP: If you and your partner each find yourselves stubbornly holding on to one potential solution ("It's you versus me!"), consider whether you are trying to reactively take control. Perhaps you're using stubborn control to cope with underlying feelings of hurt or fear? Consider working through the Four Steps (see page 95) before proceeding, and see if that helps you and your partner get creative.

Learn to Apologize Well

Apologizing well to your partner when you err in judgment is a crucial skill for relational wellness. The first step of apologizing effectively requires listening, so that you can be certain you understand the ways in which your partner was harmed and the impact of your words or actions on their feelings.

A heartfelt apology often includes three elements:

1. Direct responsibility for a specific act that resulted in pain. For example, "I'm sorry for (specific words, actions, or decisions) that led to your feeling (describe what your partner may have felt)."

2. A commitment that you will try not to hurt your partner in the same way in the future

3. A demonstration of care through changed behavior

Though apologizing well is a skill that anyone can learn, it's important to remember that even the best apologies aren't always accepted. If a "deal breaker" line is crossed, relationships are sometimes dissolved or permanently changed even after an apology has occurred.

Apologizing is often a challenging act of humility, in which a person willingly takes responsibility for their behaviors without excuses or justifications. "I'm sorry but ..." is a tempting phrase that often does more harm than good.

Those couples who do the hard work of mutually apologizing when they make errors are more likely to experience deeply satisfying relationships.

> TIP: If you become aware that your partner's feelings are hurt but don't feel as though you have done anything wrong, you can try using the active listening skills in chapter 4 (see page 55), as well as encourage mutual use of the emotional regulation skills earlier in this chapter. After practicing these strategies, you and your partner may discuss whether an apology is relevant.

Set Boundaries

Boundaries are not just about saying no; they're also about saying yes to the values and principles that matter to you. For example, valuing personal safety would require saying no to abuse in a relationship in order to say yes to safety.

How would you know if your relationship with your partner became abusive? According to the National Domestic Violence Hotline, "One feature shared by most abusive relationships is that the abusive partner tries to establish or gain power and control." Abuse isn't always physical—for example, emotional abuse may include a partner saying, "You never do anything right," preventing you from making any decisions, or insulting you in front of friends. If you find yourself in an abusive relationship, consider seeking individual therapy to assist you in setting boundaries around personal safety, such as removing yourself from the abusive relationship.

Take time to determine what values are most important to you in your relationship in addition to personal safety (consider referring back to the Morals and Values exercise on page 38). For example, if mutual respect is a significant value, identify the behaviors in your relationship that would reflect mutual respect, such as sharing feelings without interrupting each other, and the behaviors that would be counter to mutual respect, such as name-calling. Defining the lines you would like to draw in your relationship can help couples become more aware when they cross boundaries.

Write down the values that you each would like to prioritize in your relationship. What are the behaviors aligned with these values? What are the behaviors incongruent with these values? Write them down and discuss them with your partner.

If your relationship begins to exhibit behaviors that are incongruent with your values, consider actions that ensure your values are protected in the future.

SIGN OF RESPECT

Kennedy was distraught. "I expected my parents to be controlling when I was young, but I never expected this from my partner. Brooklyn said that I was wrong when I told her about my views. Wrong! As if she is the judge. My opinion is valid!"

Brooklyn shifted uncomfortably on the sofa. "I don't really understand what the issue is," she said, glancing at the therapist. "Can I not say when I think Kennedy is wrong?"

After some exploration around Kennedy's feelings, it became apparent that Kennedy didn't mind disagreement with Brooklyn, but she felt uncomfortable with the idea of Brooklyn's particular vocabulary in the conflict. After enduring years of abuse from her parents, Kennedy drew strong boundaries around respect, and Brooklyn's assertion that Kennedy was "wrong" felt disrespectful.

"What would demonstrate respect, Kennedy?" the therapist asked. "How can Brooklyn disagree with you in a respectful way, according to you?"

"It's pretty straightforward," Kennedy responded. "If we can both work on saying, 'I disagree,' rather than, 'You're wrong,' I think our relationship would be more respectful."

Brooklyn looked relieved. "I can do that. That makes sense to me."

The therapist commended both Brooklyn and Kennedy on defining boundaries around respect in their relationship. Through clarifying communication, Brooklyn and Kennedy now know how to avoid similar conflicts in the future and how to strengthen their relationship through mutual respect.

Learn to Forgive

Healthy relationships include flawed people who occasionally make errors in judgment. When both partners are committed to continuing a relationship after a conflict, it's important to learn the skill of forgiveness.

Studies reveal that couples who demonstrate forgiveness to their partner are more likely to experience happier, longer-lasting relationships. Conversely, the inability to forgive makes it challenging to compromise or resolve issues.

So how can you forgive? Consider empathizing with the other person's pain or imagining the feelings that led to their harmful behavior. Explore if their actions may have resulted from a misunderstanding or a lack of awareness about the impact of their choices. Do their choices make sense with the information they had at the time? Finally, consider the ways in which people have forgiven you for your own errors. Humbly recalling the times when you've been forgiven by others may help you graciously extend mercy to your partner.

Forgive Yourself

Forgiving yourself includes taking responsibility for your choices and accepting yourself despite errors in judgment. When you make choices that hurt your partner and then you subsequently show care through attentive listening, exploration of their needs, and changed behavior, holding on to feelings of shame won't benefit your relationship. In fact, dwelling on your inadequacies only prolongs self-focus, distracting from the important work of rebuilding a positive and healthy bond with your partner. For the benefit of your mental health and the health of your relationship, learn to do the hard work of forgiving yourself.

Couple Check-In

In this chapter, you've learned the potential benefits of conflict and the strategies for emotional regulation that can help prime you for productive conflict resolution with your partner. Equipped with tools for creating healthy boundaries, apologizing well, and forgiveness, you're now prepared to work through challenges in a mutually beneficial manner. Well done! In part 3, you will prepare for your future with your partner, navigating finances and family decisions together to create a relationship that will stand the test of time.

Building Our Future: Tools for Looking Ahead

So far in this book, you've spent time exploring your relationship with your partner and learned skills surrounding the three Cs: communication, closeness, and conflict. Next, it's time to look ahead and set goals for your shared future. In part 3, you'll be establishing how to set healthy expectations around finances, careers, and family planning and establish a commitment that lasts.

CHAPTER 7

Finances and Careers

Some couples find it difficult or awkward to discuss finances and careers, but unifying your perspectives on these topics will contribute to your relationship's commitment and longevity.

Where We Are Financially

It's important to discuss your current financial situation so that you both know your strengths and challenges as you set goals for your shared future. Honest conversations with your partner about money prepare your relationship for mutual trust, vulnerability, and intimacy.

Disclosing financial missteps, creating financial goals, and evaluating financial habits are all responsible practices for couples who are ready to take their relationship to the next level. Though finances aren't always easy to discuss, consider the alternative: Do you really want to risk unforeseen financial hazards? For better or for worse, your partner's financial choices will likely impact your relationship at some point. This chapter offers an opportunity to work toward the life you want to build with your partner using the tools of careers and money.

For most people, finances are emotional. Before delving into the details of your finances, take time to identify which challenging emotions you may associate with money and career choices:

Anger	Fear	Irresponsibility	Shame
Anxiety	Guilt	Irritation	Worry
Confusion	Humiliation	Loss	
Envy	Insufficiency	Sadness	

By confronting difficult emotions around finances head-on, you and your partner can openly assess the validity of financial fears, consider moral convictions around money, and resist the avoidance that shame thrives on.

Before proceeding, turn to your partner and make a commitment toward empathy, agreeing to practice consideration for each other's feelings of pain around money. Decide in advance what your plan will be if you find yourselves in conflict as you discuss the topics of this chapter. Will you take a break? Will you practice emotional grounding, as discussed in chapter 6? Will you seek a financial or counseling professional as an objective third party? Even if you anticipate a smooth discussion, being prepared doesn't hurt!

Finances are all about the long game. By enduring short-term stress or boredom about the topic, you'll work through challenges that could otherwise prevent you from ensuring a financially stable life for you and your loved ones.

Spending and Saving Habits

How did your caregivers handle money? Was money taboo, or was it openly discussed? Who controlled the money in your home? How important was money? What were the unspoken rules about money? Behaviors and habits around money can be formed by age seven, according to a study out of Cambridge University in 2013. Take some time to identify and discuss the habits and patterns modeled by your family of origin from the time you were a child.

Next, consider the stories or ideas around money that shaped your family's habits. For example, if your parent had a traumatic job loss, you may have been taught to work extra hard at a job out of fear that it could disappear at any moment. Or if your family was image-conscious, money may have felt vital to social status. What did your parents' careers or financial choices teach you about money?

Money is a symbol; what does it represent to you? Do your perceptions around money lend themselves more to saving or spending? For example, if money represents security for you, you may be inclined toward saving money for retirement. If money represents status to you, you may be prone to spending money on lifestyle purchases.

Circle the top three associations that you have with the acquisition of money. Discuss your reflections with your partner.

Attraction: Having money draws people to me or allows me to woo people.

Confidence: Having money helps me feel confident and assured.

Freedom: Having money allows me to experience freedom with time, spending, or other choices.

Generosity: Having money allows me to give to people in need.

Independence: Having money allows me to be self-sufficient.

Legacy: Having money serves as a legacy for future generations or charities.

Play: Having money funds hobbies or interests that foster happiness.

Power: Having money provides me with the influence that I crave.

Responsibility: Having money means I am responsible and mature.

Rest: Having money provides opportunities for relaxation.

Security: Having money means I am safe and secure.

Self-Worth: Having money means I am worthy of love or respect.

Status: Having money gives me access to an image and lifestyle I desire.

Tool: Having money means I have a tool that can be used as a resource for a number of helpful purposes.

Tradition: Having money provides for a traditional way of life, such as caring for future generations.

Banking and Bills

Your relationship might be an equal commitment, but your monetary contributions could be more complicated. What do you do if you make more money than your partner—do you still split the bills? What if you're paying off student loans? How do you account for child support payments or an employer matching your 401(k) contributions? Figuring out how to share money or split bills can be a headache!

Developing a plan for banking and bills that works for your relationship is important, yet there's not a single model or plan that works for everybody. Take the quiz below to discover your preferred strategy for your relationship with your partner:

1. Do you want your money to be kept in …

    a. An individual bank account
    b. A joint account with your partner
    c. Partially in an individual account and partially in a shared account (for example, bills may be paid from a joint account, and "fun money" may be kept in individual accounts)

2. Do you think bills should be split …

    a. 50/50
    b. At a percentage according to our income. For example, if I make $45k and my partner makes $55k, I would pay 45 percent of the bills and my partner would pay 55 percent of the bills.
    c. By taking responsibility for various categories. For example, I may pay rent because my partner pays for health insurance.
    d. Bills will not be split because one of us is not expected or able to work.

3. When unexpected expenses occur (for example, the water bill is higher due to a leak), who will pay?

   a. The bill will continue to be split or shared by an agreed-upon percentage.
   b. The partner who is most responsible for the expense will pay.
   c. Both my partner and I will contribute to a mutual emergency account as we are able.
   d. One partner will pay for any unexpected expenses.

WHAT ARE YOU COMFORTABLE GIVING?

Quinn and Val were months from marriage when Quinn mentioned $50,000 of deferred student debt.

"I'm not sure what to do," Val reflected in a session. "I thought that we would split our bills down the middle, but I'm not sure how Quinn is going to be able to afford that when the student loan payments kick in. That's going to cost more than our rent! We're vowing to commit to each other 'for richer or poorer,' so I feel like I should help out with my savings, especially since I have a higher salary. But I don't want to get resentful ..."

"Resentment is a feeling that comes up when people feel like they're giving more than they're comfortable," their therapist noted. "What are you comfortable giving?"

"I'm happy to split our bills according to the difference in our salaries," Val said. "It's not Quinn's fault that adjunct professors are underpaid! But I don't feel good about paying for all of Quinn's student debt right now because I just finished paying off my student loans, and I'm worried that I'll start our marriage off feeling upset—even though I haven't even been asked to pay for the student loans."

Their therapist affirmed Val for looking out for the health and well-being of their marriage and provided a reference to a financial adviser. Emotional vulnerability makes the topic of money easy to avoid, but honest disclosures about financial concerns help couples focus on the necessary next steps toward financial responsibility.

Budgeting and Debt

Managing money can feel like a full-time job for some couples. The stress of staying on top of bills, unexpected expenses, investments, savings, and debt management can cause conflict for some couples and avoidance for others. A Debt.com survey revealed that, as of 2019, 33 percent of Americans didn't maintain a budget at all, though 80 percent of Americans carry debt such as car loans, student loans, credit card balances, or mortgages.

For the health and stability of your relationship, it's important to define expectations and roles around financial management. Take the quiz below and discuss the results with your partner.

1. Who will own paying bills and managing budgets?

    a. We will assign one of us to own bill pay and budget management.
    b. We will collaborate on all bills and meet for regular budget meetings.
    c. We will each pay bills and manage budgets separately.

2. How will budgetary issues be addressed?

    a. The assigned budget manager will alert the partner of changes that must be made to the budget or spending/saving habits.
    b. The individual with a concern will ask for a relationship finance meeting to discuss an issue together and make a mutual plan for resolution.
    c. Budgetary issues will not be addressed because our finances will be kept totally separate and personal.

3. Who is expected to pay for long-term goals, such as a house, schooling for a potential child, or retirement?

    a. We are not saving for long-term goals.
    b. Both my partner and I share these responsibilities. (Get specific. For example, are both partners depositing the same amount of money or the same percentage of their earnings?)
    c. Our savings are considered personal decisions rather than relationship decisions.
    d. One person in the relationship is responsible for saving for long-term goals.

4. Who will manage investments?

    a. We will assign one of us to manage investments, trusting their expertise or resourcefulness.
    b. We will collaborate on our investment strategies—all decisions about investing will be shared.
    c. We will each manage investments personally.
    d. We will entrust a financial professional to manage our investments.

5. Who will pay for individual debts, such as student loan debt or personal credit card debt?

    a. We will evenly split all debts.
    b. We will keep debts separate and pay for our own.
    c. We will pay a percentage of debts, according to our incomes.
    d. We will decide which debts to share and which debts to keep separate.

QUESTIONS FOR DISCUSSION

1. What's most important to you in your budget?
2. What expenses do you want to prioritize?
3. What expenditures are least important to you in your budget?

Long-Term Goals

Buying a home, having children, and retiring all require financial planning. Your long-term goals may be as unique as your relationship, but the importance of honesty and communication is critical no matter what visions you have for the future.

With your partner, consider the list of significant financial goals below. Write your estimated savings goal and desired timeline next to each objective that's applicable to you or your partner.

OBJECTIVE	AMOUNT OF $ REQUIRED	TIMELINE
Build an emergency savings fund		
Buy or lease a car		
Buy a home		
Donate or give away money		
Fund a legacy project		
Go on vacation		
Have children		
Invest		
Pay off debt		
Save for education or career investments		
Rent a home		

Save for children's education		
Save for retirement		
Save for a remodel		

Careers and Occupations

Jobs and vocations may change over time, but supporting each other through your daily work is key. Transitions will surely occur, whether in job title or status; the U.S. Bureau of Labor estimates that adults hold an average of 12 jobs over the course of their lifetime, often with varying periods of unemployment. While transitions are often stressful, they tend to be necessary for building financial and occupational growth—would you really want to stay in the same job you had as a teenager for the rest of your life? In this section, you'll develop strategies for dealing with relationship expectations around career choices, job loss, work/life balance, household roles, and shared holidays or vacations. Hold your partner's hand and get ready to dig into some hot topics!

Objectives and Expectations around Career

It's essential to discuss your objectives and expectations for both your and your partner's occupations early in your committed relationship. Consider the following questions to ensure that you're on the same page:

1. Do you expect yourself and/or your partner to remain in the job you have now for any particular length of time?

2. Do you feel that there are elements outside either of your control that may impact job stability or trajectory?

3. Do you have expectations for you or your partner to achieve a particular education level, job title, or pay rate/salary?

4. Do you anticipate potential moves for you or your partner related to job or education opportunities?

5. What objectives do you have for each of your careers? For example, is there a goal to meaningfully help a certain population, reach a particular financial goal, or experience job satisfaction?

6. Do you have a sense of meaning or purpose regarding your career or vocation?

PERSONAL GROWTH CAN BE CONTAGIOUS

"I am so proud of your hard work, honey—you did it! You got your master's degree! But I just never considered that we would have to move..."

Sadie and Carlos had just finished a long road together: Their entire relationship had navigated years of schooling and internships. They had every reason to celebrate, especially since Sadie had been offered her dream job right after graduation. The only problem? It was across the country, in a state Carlos and Sadie had never even visited.

"There's so much to consider," Carlos sighed. "I don't know if my company has offices in that state. What if I have to give up my job so that Sadie can have her dream job? And what if her dream job ends up being less than ideal? I knew that our relationship would include sacrifices, but this is a tough one."

"I don't want you to go if you're not happy going," Sadie said tearfully. "I understand if you need to stay here."

"The funny thing is, I don't know that I do want to stay here," Carlos said with a laugh. "I just never considered a different life than the one we had. All I knew for years was the consistency of my familiar job, your schooling, and our hometown."

After a few months of dreaming and planning, Sadie and Carlos decided to move across the country for Sadie's new job, while Carlos began an academic program in a neighboring city to pursue growth in his career. "It didn't feel right to choose one of our futures," Carlos said in our last session. "I expect both of us to thrive. Sadie's success helped me realize that I had delayed my own professional growth for years."

By mutually reflecting on their vocations, professional goals, and expectations for themselves and their relationship, Sadie and Carlos challenged themselves and spurred each other toward fulfilling accomplishments. When it comes to relationships, personal growth can be contagious.

Job Losses

Your relationship loses more than a paycheck when job loss strikes. Monetary stressors aside, job loss often results in emotional and relational challenges for both partners. Feelings like embarrassment, worry, anger, and disappointment are common during periods of unemployment, sometimes leading to depression, anxiety, and poor self-esteem. Despite all the difficulties that come with losing a job, your relationship can be a source of necessary support when times are tough.

How do you and your partner manage unexpected changes? Transitioning to a new schedule, routine, standard of living, budget, and status can be stressful, yet change brings opportunity as well. Unemployment may offer a chance for you and your partner to reevaluate how you spend your time and money, where you live, your chosen career fields, and your household roles and responsibilities.

Once you and/or your partner are ready to begin a new job search, it can be helpful to create a strategy early in the process. Discuss expectations around how much time will be spent job-searching and applying as well as how much time will be spent on other household responsibilities. Plan when you'll discuss the job-search process and budgetary concerns so that stressors don't seep into every facet of your life.

It's likely that you didn't start dating your partner because of their job or paycheck, so try to remember what attracted you to each other. For example, if your relationship was built on friendship, take time to reconnect on a deeper level. If you felt passionately attracted, nurture intimacy in your relationship. If the two of you can transform a season of unemployment into a renewal of your relationship, all is not lost.

> TIP: Identify activities, dates, and excursions that don't require much money. Consider integrating these activities into your shared lives on a regular basis as a reminder that you can have fun without financial pressure.

Roles at Home

There are countless tasks that keep homes running: laundry, dishes, planning doctor appointments, mowing the lawn, school pickups, repairing cars, scrubbing toilets, and more. Completing household tasks is a form of unpaid labor, so it's important that you and your partner negotiate how to fairly divide these chores to avoid the pain of resentment later.

Though some couples choose not to designate particular tasks and "wing it," my experience as a relationship therapist has taught me that undefined roles can sometimes lead to unfair and unnoticed burdens on one partner.

To begin the process of dividing household roles, discuss the following questions:

1. Are there chores, objects, or responsibilities that are particularly important to you? For example, are you passionate about upkeep of the car or the way laundry is done?

2. Can you think of chores or activities that may be dependent on, or related to, other chores? Cleaning the kitchen, grocery shopping, cooking, and doing the dishes are all related chores.

3. Are there childcare or job responsibilities that one partner holds more than another partner?

4. Are there mental responsibilities that are difficult to quantify in time but require regular attention from a partner? For example, if a partner is responsible for monitoring a child's education, discuss the energy, stress, or "mental load" required for that task when assessing fair division of labor.

5. Discuss whether you and your partner would like to use the chore division method below. If not, discuss an alternative method for household management that appeals to you both.

- Make a list of all the chores that need to get done weekly, monthly, and annually, noting the approximate time each chore takes or the amount of effort required.

- Place related chores in the same categories. Divide the chore categories evenly, or choose a different ratio if that is "fairer" based on your current childcare and/or job responsibilities.

- Choose chore categories based on your interests, values, and pickiness (e.g., rather than micromanaging your partner's method for loading the dishwasher, volunteer to take over the kitchen category).

- Plan a time to evaluate how the division of labor is feeling for both of you, considering whether you would like to rotate roles or stick to your chosen categories.

DEFINE YOUR DOMESTIC TERRITORY

"Are you seriously not going to separate colors in the laundry?"

"Are you ever going to do the dishes?"

Dana and Bailey were constantly bickering. Though they had agreed to share all the responsibilities after moving in together, they couldn't seem to agree on how and when the chores should get done. Both Dana and Bailey felt like they were overworked, underappreciated, and fed up with their partner.

After some discussion, their therapist determined that what Dana and Bailey yearned for was ownership. Both partners wanted to manage the timeliness and method of chore completion in their apartment, but since they lacked a clear division of responsibilities, they sometimes overlooked their own chores to micromanage their partner.

"Dana, what's your territory?" their therapist asked during session. "You're going to be in charge of this territory, so you'll need to be responsible for everything in it."

"Well, I'm very particular about paying our bills on time and I check twice when Bailey pays them out, so I'll take the finance domain: budgeting, bill pay, investing, and paying taxes."

"Bailey, what about you?"

"Well, I'm tired of seeing dirty dishes in the sink, so I'm going to take over the kitchen territory," Bailey said. "I'll do the grocery shopping, kitchen cleaning, food preparation, and dishes."

Over the next few weeks, Bailey and Dana took proud ownership in their chosen territories. Rather than procrastinating due to lack of oversight from their partner, they instead became more efficient in their completion of chores.

"When I noticed some plates in the sink yesterday, instead of getting angry with Dana, I knew that the mess was my responsibility," shared Bailey. "So I got to it. Dishes felt less emotionally loaded, and I kind of enjoyed getting into the flow of it. Plus, I knew that the dinner I was excited to make was reliant on me getting the dishes done."

Territory planning paid off for Dana and Bailey, focusing their attention on the chore territories within their full control and creating opportunities for self-motivation according to their chosen interests.

Work/Life Balance

Though work can provide financially and offer a sense of purpose, it's helpful to slow down and consider whether other values and important relationships are receiving enough attention as well. Do you know who or what you're working for? Are you living a life that's sustainable and healthy for you, your partner, and any people who may be dependent on you? When was the last time you "shut off" from work or responsibilities to rest and recover?

Underworking and overworking can both be signs of underlying mental health challenges such as depression and anxiety. If you find yourself wanting to work more or less but feel unable to shift that dial, you might consider seeking therapeutic help to assist you in discerning the root causes of your behavior.

If the pressures of financial or career goals create relational strain for you and your partner, spend a day together with the express purpose of playing and immersing yourself in something outside of responsibilities, like rambling in nature, painting, or swimming. Draw your attention to the joys in the moment, particularly taking note of delights that occur without your effort. Therapists sometimes remind clients that "we're all the ages we ever were," and the childlike parts of you and your partner may need to help you two attune to the freedom and joy of the present. After all, the best things in life are free.

QUESTIONS FOR DISCUSSION

Think of a time when you felt totally relaxed. What was the context surrounding that rest?

Now think of a time when you felt purposeful and fulfilled. What provided that sense of drive and meaning?

Couple Check-In

Nice work! You've navigated a sensitive topic that's notoriously challenging for many couples to discuss. By communicating about budgets, debts, spending, saving, careers, and household responsibilities at this stage in your commitment, you and your partner are laying a foundation for direct, honest, and respectful dialogue for years to come. In the next chapter, you'll explore the topic of relationships beyond the two of you, determining the kind of bond you would like to share with family members, friends, and possibly children.

CHAPTER 8

Family Beyond Us Two

In this chapter, you'll learn how to navigate the topics of having children and relationships with family members and friends. The role other people play in your relationship is important to discuss at this stage of your commitment. The strategies outlined in this chapter will assist you and your partner in having productive conversations that propel you toward a thriving relationship.

Growing Our Family

Discussing your desires and expectations about having children is fundamental as you and your partner plan your future together. Making sure you are sincerely aligned in your feelings about whether to expand your family together requires honesty, transparency, and nonjudgment. You may discover that you have differing plans or viewpoints, but acknowledging your partner's perspective through active listening doesn't mean you have to agree. Consider focusing on mutual understanding in this chapter before seeking harmony about whether to grow your family.

"Do you want to have children?" can feel like a loaded question—and it is. When couples decide to have children, they are committing to a lifetime of shared work and responsibility, well beyond 18 years. Consider adding nuance to this blunt inquiry by discussing the following questions with your partner:

1. What is your vocation—the meaningful work that you feel equipped to complete in life?

2. What do you hope your legacy will be?

3. Does raising children fit in with your desired vocation and legacy?

4. Do you have experience with children, positive or negative?

5. How do you envision co-parenting if you decide to have children?

6. What lifestyle standards or principles are you unwilling to compromise if you choose to have children?

7. What challenges might arise in having children due to differences in our racial, cultural, socioeconomic, or religious backgrounds?

8. What would you want to replicate from your upbringing if you have children, and what would you want to leave in the past?

9. What are your biggest fears about parenting?

10. What are your greatest hopes about parenting?

PROJECTING THE FUTURE

Emma and Kevin were expecting their first child. "We're so excited!" Emma said, smiling. "I can't wait to see our child's graduation at the church preschool that I went to as a kid."

"Oh, right," Kevin began. "I wanted to talk to you about that. I think we should put our kid in a Mandarin immersion school. I want them to be fluent in Mandarin so they can talk to my family, and it's easiest to teach them when they're young."

Emma's face fell. "Wait, what? I don't speak Mandarin. How is this going to work?"

"Well, you could learn Mandarin, too. There are some great apps now."

Their therapist cut in to ease some of the building tension. "Kevin, tell me more about the vision you have for your child. What are you feeling and thinking?"

"I could never talk with my aunts and grandma," Kevin disclosed. "I was raised in the United States and didn't know Mandarin until adulthood. The language barrier between me and my extended family as a child felt awkward to me. I'm hoping my child could have a different experience and learn about their heritage."

"Emma, what are you feeling?" the therapist probed.

"I'm in a fog. I always pictured our child as being like me as a child, and I didn't know Mandarin. I feel like I'm reimagining the future, and I have no idea what it looks like."

The therapist encouraged Emma and Kevin to close their eyes and imagine their child in a number of educational settings and experiences. After a few minutes, she asked how the exercise felt.

"It's so funny," Emma began. "I felt nervous about the Mandarin school, and I pictured myself anxious as our kid walked up the steps of the school away from us. And then when I tried to picture each of the other school options, I had the exact same feeling—nervous for our child to walk away from us. I can't keep this baby in my womb forever, but it's scary to lose control. The preschool I went to as a child felt safe, like a known entity. The reality is, parenting is going to be full of unknowns and new territories."

Kevin nodded. "I realized that I wanted to protect our child from the challenges I faced as a child, but I can't do that. Our child will have challenges regardless, so the best thing we can do is get to know them first and make decisions out of our love for them."

The therapist commended Kevin and Emma on communicating their fears and refraining from the temptation to project their anxieties and personal histories onto their child. When the baby was born, both Emma and Kevin were dutifully attentive to the particular needs and experiences of their baby from day one.

Number and Timing

"We want kids someday" is a common reflection among couples, but when it comes down to the decision about when and how many, couples sometimes find themselves less in agreement. Consider these questions to help you and your partner open up about possible child-rearing preferences:

1. How many children do you think you would like to raise, if any?

2. Are there financial, educational, career, or personal goals that you would like to accomplish before having children?

3. Are there elements in your life, such as drug or alcohol abuse, that would be unsafe for a child to be around?

4. Are there skills you want to learn that would help you feel competent to raise a child?

5. Who do you envision would be responsible as the primary caregiver of a child? For example, would childcare be split between you and your partner? Would one person need to quit their job? Would childcare or extended family be used for babysitting?

6. What kind of sibling relationships do you consider to be ideal? For example, would you prefer playmates close in age or an older sibling who can mentor or assist with a younger sibling?

7. Are you aware of potential challenges with fertility if you hope to conceive, including age or health considerations?

8. If you hope to conceive, when do you envision removing barriers to conception (contraceptives)?

9. Are you concerned about the potential of having a child with disabilities?

Blended Families, Fostering, and Adoption

There are countless ways to grow a family, including welcoming a stepchild from a prior relationship, fostering, or adopting.

If your partner already has children, thoughtfully consider whether you are prepared for the effort, sacrifices, and potential joys of child-rearing. After all, considering whether you are ready to commit to the responsibilities of step-parenthood is a separate question from whether you are ready to commit to your partner. Developing comfort and a sense of belonging for all members of a blended family often takes time, though joy abounds when couples are prepared and committed for this step in their family relationships.

If you are considering a blended family:

1. What values do you share with potential stepchildren? For example, are you and your potential stepchild both animal and nature lovers? Do you both value family time?
2. What activities or interests could be developed from those shared values? For example, could you train a pet together? Go on hikes? Join an educational wilderness group?
3. What relationship may be expected between you and other parent figures?
4. What relationship activities or involvement may be expected between you, your partner, and current children, considering the ages, developmental needs, and possible preferences of the children?
5. What boundaries would be respected between you and the potential stepchildren to create a sense of security and stability for them? For example, would you be expected to discipline the children? Would children be permitted to choose their expressions of affection, such as hugs or high-fives?

Fostering and/or adopting with your partner may include special considerations about how to best support potential children. Consider the following questions for discussion if you and your partner hope to foster or adopt a child:

1. What is your drive or hope in fostering or adopting a child?
2. What is your comfort with possible unknowns regarding a child's trauma, health, or genetic background?
3. What are some qualities that you notice in yourself or your partner that may be particularly beneficial to the foster/adoption journey (e.g., flexibility, perseverance, empathy, etc.)?
4. Do you have any discomfort about caring for a child who may have experienced trauma, abuse, neglect, or exposure to illicit substances?
5. Are you open to collaboration and/or co-parenting with biological parents, a foster/adoption agency, and/or a therapeutic care team?

6. What are circumstances that you may or may not be open to regarding fostering or adoption? For example:

   a. Are you open to domestic and international adoption?
   b. Are you interested in open and closed adoption?
   c. Are you willing to parent children from different biological families?
   d. Are you inclined to parent children of various ages and racial ethnic backgrounds and provide them with a support network that shares their heritage?
   e. Are you prepared to commit to understanding issues regarding racial privilege, bias, and discrimination that may impact your child?
   f. Are you able to commit to cultural education about a child's racial and ethnic background?

A SHARED COMMITMENT

Sudhir and Mia came to therapy confused and distraught. They had hoped for children but were struggling with years of infertility after a number of miscarriages. Doctors couldn't give them concrete answers or explanations. Their relationship felt like it was at a standstill.

"We always talked about having two kids, a dog, and a house. Now what?" Mia began. "I feel disconnected from Sudhir. Actually, I feel disconnected from everyone."

"And I feel rejected. Why can't we just enjoy each other?" remarked Sudhir. 'We had a really enjoyable relationship; I think we should build on that."

As Mia worked through her grief, Sudhir learned to care empathetically for Mia's lost dreams. Asking her to share, Sudhir learned to listen and hold Mia's pain even though it felt so different from his hope for the future.

"I know that having biological children was what we planned on, but I want to be a mother," Mia shared one day. "Sudhir, are you willing to talk about adoption?"

Sudhir looked uncertain. "I don't know the first thing about adoption. How it works, how much it costs, how long the process is ..."

Mia looked crestfallen, then angry. "You know how hard it was for me to miscarry. I can't believe you're not willing to adopt."

"Mia," their therapist said gently, "I know that you're feeling vulnerable. It was a big risk to ask Sudhir about adoption. You're afraid. But I want you to listen to what Sudhir is saying. He simply needs more information before he can make a decision. Are you willing to help him with that?"

Mia's shoulders fell. "Yes. Of course. It's hard not to be afraid after so much loss. Sudhir, I have a friend who adopted. Let's meet up with her and find out more so that you can have the information you need."

Sudhir and Mia eventually decided to adopt, but it took them time to get on the same page. They each had their own emotions, hopes, and expectations surrounding their future. When they finally welcomed a child into their family, they were unified and steady, having honored their own feelings and reservations until they felt comfortable with the commitment of parenting together.

Parenting Styles and Responsibilities

Discussing parenting styles before having children sets you up for success by clarifying expectations and shared goals. For example, one partner might expect to run a family with a strict parental hierarchy while the other prefers to let their kids roam free. It's better to work through these challenges early in your commitment, so you can discuss the potential benefits and consequences, identify values behind parenting choices, and build trust by having mutual consent.

Developmental psychologist Diana Baumrind sorted parenting styles into three primary categories—authoritative parenting, authoritarian parenting, and permissive parenting—noting a correlation between parenting styles and the resulting behavior of children. To discover your parenting style, take the quiz below:

1. How should decisions be made in families?

    a. Kids should feel empowered to make most of their decisions.
    b. Parents need to lead—they are in charge, children are not.
    c. Parents should provide guidelines but also listen to their children's concerns.

2. How do you feel about rules in families?

    a. Kids shouldn't have rules. Freedom is important.
    b. Parents should be strict with kids. Expectations yield results.
    c. Parents should provide direction with clear explanations to help kids learn.

3. How should parents respond when kids disagree with them?

    a. Kids are strong and smart. Let them do what they think is best.
    b. It's important not to let children talk back to their parents.
    c. Kids should have a say in how families are run, but parents are ultimately responsible to choose what's best for their family.

If you chose mostly As, you may have a permissive parenting style: You have few expectations for your potential children, valuing their autonomy. Your potential children may view you more as a friend than as a parent.

If you chose mostly Bs, you may have an authoritarian parenting style: You have high expectations for obedience and conformity from your children, perhaps drawing from the concept of tough love. You may anticipate setting firm rules for your future children with little wiggle room.

If you chose mostly Cs, you may have an authoritative parenting style: You have expectations for your potential children, but you also hope to be responsive to their ideas. Boundaries and rule-setting may result from intentional dialogue between you and your future children, creating a democracy in your household.

Education

Most parents want the best for their children, but what does it mean to provide the best education? The questions below will help you and your partner develop a shared vision to guide educational decisions in the future.

QUESTIONS FOR DISCUSSION

1. What are your educational goals for potential children? Do you expect your children to attend college or a trade school? If you or your partner pursued higher education, do you expect your potential children to follow suit?
2. Will you and your partner share responsibility for schoolwork and activities throughout your children's education?
3. Are you or your partner interested in alternative educational styles, such as homeschooling? Are you anticipating that future children may attend public schools or private schools?
4. What are your hopes or visions for the development of your potential children? For example, do you hope they develop a love of learning or create effective change in the world around them? Do you hope for academic success? To what end or purpose?

In-Laws, Siblings, and Extended Family

Your level of interaction with extended family members in your relationship isn't entirely up to you and your partner, but it can be helpful to discuss the degree of connection that you each anticipate.

As you and your partner develop your relationship, you will benefit from establishing some boundaries with other family members. For example, some couples establish boundaries by moving out of a parent's house or moving to a new location. Others establish boundaries by limiting the advice they internalize from family members, instead relying on their relationship to make important decisions.

Determine the difference between helpful insight or help from family members versus intrusion into your relationship. While extended family may be a wonderful source of support and community for many couples, at times they may also place strain on otherwise stable relationships. Explore the potential strengths and challenges of extended family relationships with the discussion questions below:

1. Do your parents, siblings, or extended family members offer meaningful support for your relationship? Do you enjoy participating in their lives and/or caring for their needs?

2. What kinds of cultural, emotional, relational, or financial participation is expected in your extended family?

3. Do you feel obligated or responsible for your parents, siblings, or extended family? Do you expect your partner to caretake for your extended family or participate in their lives? How and when?

4. Do you often feel hurt, sad, or anxious around family members? Do you regress or feel you're treated like a child? Are there boundaries you would like to establish with your partner in how you interact with your family?

5. Are there ways that you and your partner may wish to establish privacy or independence from extended family in certain areas (e.g., are there topics that are off-limits for extended family)?

"Every Christmas we all go to the lake, and then every Easter we all go to the desert," Donan shared. "And then in the summer we all go to Hawaii."

The therapist glanced at Donan's partner Billy, who looked tired.

"And then on Sunday nights, we go to her parents' house for barbecues," Billy added, resigned.

"Tell me what you're thinking, Billy," the therapist encouraged.

"It's just that I thought we would grow out of that. When we first started dating, we were in high school. Now we're adults, but we spend just as much time with Donan's family as ever. When will we have our own vacations—or weekends, for that matter?"

"I didn't know you felt that way, Billy." Donan reached out, taking his hand. "It feels so natural to me, of course—it's my family. I don't want to force you to go on all these trips and dinners, but I really love my family. Should we just stay home?"

"No," Billy quickly responded. "I want you to enjoy time with your family. Your love for your family is one of the things I respect about you; I would never take that away. I just don't want to spend as much time with them as you do."

The therapist commended Billy for honestly sharing his feelings and desires with Donan. "So, Billy, it sounds like you don't want to spend as much time with Donan's family, but you're encouraging her to keep her relationship with her family close. And you also want time that's set apart for you and Donan to relax or make new memories together, is that right?"

"Yes, I've felt this way for a while, but I always felt selfish asking. It sounds all right now that we're saying it out loud."

Donan laughed. "I wish you'd shared sooner! I'm totally fine with a change. I love you and am open to us taking our weekends for ourselves. I'm even okay with creating new holiday traditions, but I'll probably be pretty sad if we miss Christmas with Grandma this year."

Ironically, as the couple pulled back from Donan's family, Billy's relationship with his in-laws flourished. "I feel excited to see them again," Billy said. "I think I was tired of seeing them so often and felt resentful that I was stuck in a rut. Now that we're choosing when to go to their house, I feel more connected."

Donan and Billy honored flexibility in their relationship with in-laws, adapting their involvement to their own relationship's needs and their individual preferences.

Friends

One of the topics I am passionate about as a relationship therapist is the importance of building a community of support around relationships, ideally with a network of mutual friends. Individuals or fellow couples who are peers or mentors offer countless benefits to committed couples by normalizing relational challenges and modeling healthy dynamics.

When my husband and I were in graduate school, we had weekly dinners with other newlywed couples who informed the way we relate to each other to this day. Our conversations often focused on the qualities that attracted us to our spouses, their quirks, and the challenges we faced in merging our lives together. Over time, we naturally began to mirror one another: As Lauren was often patient with George, I would find myself patient with my husband. Because Donovan was often willing to opine differently than his wife Emily in discussions, my husband learned to respectfully challenge my perspective. Couples tend to subconsciously mimic and reflect the people around them, so why not choose positively influential people to surround your relationship in this early stage of commitment?

Another benefit to sharing some friendships with your partner is that it limits the risk of skewed, one-sided perspectives when disclosing relational challenges. Family members and friends of one partner in a relationship may more readily validate the perspective of that individual rather than working to understand the other partner's perspective. Shared friends (or third parties, such as therapists) may be more likely to consider both sides of a challenge, normalize typical difficulties, inspire options for resolution, and consider options that benefit the relationship as a whole.

QUESTIONS FOR DISCUSSION

1. Who are the six friends with whom you spend the most time? Do they embody characteristics that could benefit your relationship with your partner?
2. Who are the friends you and your partner have in common? Do those friends positively influence how you relate to each other?
3. What forms of relational support might you seek from friendships? Are you and your partner comfortable sharing about your relationship to friends? If so, who? Are there topics that are off-limits or private?

Couple Check-In

In this chapter, you and your partner have discussed important questions surrounding if and how you would like to grow your family. Now that you have clarified how you would like to expand your family, parenting styles and responsibilities, and the roles of extended family in your partnership, you are prepared for whatever the future may bring. In the next chapter, I'll address how to trust the commitment you've made with your partner and maintain your connection for years to come.

CHAPTER 9

Making It Last

You and your partner are committed to making your relationship last, so you're building your future with tools that will keep your relationship on track. In this chapter, you and your partner will honor and trust the commitment you've made with strategies for tracking your goals and reconnecting when times get tough.

Trusting Our Commitment

In a world where casual relationships are increasingly common, you and your partner have decided to commit to each other. You know that having a partner by your side through joys and difficulties requires sacrifice and hard work, but nevertheless, you are committed.

How can you and your partner learn to trust your commitment? By fully knowing and loving each other, working through conflict, and having faith in the midst of change.

Over time, you'll have countless opportunities to demonstrate curiosity and compassion to each other, reaffirming that you are both known and loved just as you are. Conflicts may arise as you both advocate for the kind of relationship you most desire and work through past pains. But you'll have many chances to practice loyalty and fidelity amid changing seasons and identities.

Tracking Our Goals

A healthy relationship is a growing relationship, so one of the best ways to keep your relationship healthy is to plan for continued growth toward values and objectives.

Discuss with your partner where you want your relationship to be in one year, five years, and 10 years.

Shift the conversation to your shared goals for your relationship, considering aspirations for physical, relational, spiritual, and mental health; finances; family growth; travel; service; and vocations.

Make sure to identify SMART goals for the best chance of success. SMART goals, developed by author Peter Drucker, include the following qualities:

Specific. For example, rather than committing to "financial responsibility," a specific goal might be, "creating our budget and meeting with a financial adviser."

Measurable. For example, "Going on one date night each week for the next year." You need to know whether the goal has been met, and adding a quantity helps assess that outcome.

Actionable. No abstract ideas here! What actions are you and your partner going to take to make sure your goal becomes reality?

Realistic. For example, a goal to have "no conflicts" is a setup for failure, but "finding a conflict resolution strategy that helps us have productive conflicts" is within anyone's means.

Time-bound. Having a deadline helps make your goals an actuality and sets the timeline for when your shared goals will be evaluated or reconfigured.

One of the most enjoyable aspects of committed relationships is the ability to make big dreams a reality through shared effort and accountability. Your future begins today!

Reconnecting and Reconnecting Again

Long-term relationships are just that: long. Even if you and your partner feel that you are starting to drift away from each other, you can always choose to reconnect and find your way back to each other.

Initiate Nurturing and Affection

"If only my partner would pursue me ..."

"I want to be wanted ..."

"I feel like I'm falling out of love ..."

The yearnings for connection that are most common in long-term committed relationships often link to feelings of helplessness. When individuals perceive their partner—or even their feelings—as the guide in their relationship, they disempower themselves to make intentional choices for connection.

By taking the initiative to enact the kind of relationship you *wish* you had, you may find that you can build that fantasy into a reality. For example, if you feel disconnected from your partner, kick off a date by reminiscing about times when you felt deeply connected and loved. Consider the elements that allowed for connection to thrive in the past and attempt to recreate those elements in the context of your current lives. Practice affection by nurturing your partner with affirming compliments and tender touch. Take control of the stagnation in your relationship by initiating connection and reintroducing the fondness that first drew you together.

REKINDLING THE FLAME

Manny and Ericka both felt worn down by life. Manny missed Ericka's carefree spirit before responsibilities seemed to take over, and Ericka missed the romantic, affectionate man she remembered when they first started dating. Both of them felt like they were victims of adulthood and a stale relationship.

"If you woke up tomorrow and you felt close and connected in your relationship, what would have changed?" the therapist prodded them.

"Well, Ericka would be on vacation from her high-pressure job, and we wouldn't open our computers or phones all day," Manny said. "We would go to our favorite restaurant and spa and spend the evening together."

"What about you, Ericka?"

"Manny's idea sounds pretty good to me! Except I would add that he would wake me up with snuggles, hold my hand and kiss me the way he used to all day long, and he would leave a love note under my pillow after we went to bed—he did that once a long time ago, and I felt so loved."

"What's holding you back from following through with this plan?" the therapist asked.

Both Manny and Ericka laughed. "Oh, a thousand things," Manny said. "Work projects, chores, deadlines."

"When you consistently choose other responsibilities over your relationship, you're saying that the relationship isn't as important," the therapist challenged them. "Consider following through with this."

Ericka and Manny took the advice, and reported back that they were glad that they did. The world didn't fall apart on their day off, and they were surprised at how easily they rekindled their relationship when responsibilities took a back seat. No longer victims of an unhappy life, Ericka and Manny took responsibility for the change they desired.

Fold in New Experiences

Years ago, I babysat for a well-respected couple in our community who had recently had their third child. They giggled as they raced out the door for a date night, placing their new baby in my arms. When they returned, I noticed that the demure mother had pierced her nose. "I was feeling kind of stale," she shared. "I needed to feel alive."

Before I became a relationship therapist, I was convinced that conflict was the primary strain on relationships. But in the decade I've spent specializing in the psychology of thriving relationships, I've become convinced that perceived disconnection and distance are far more common culprits of relationship challenges.

New experiences freshen a relationship that has grown heavy or distant with responsibility. If you and your partner begin to feel like roommates or business partners, consider indulging harmless impulses together. For example, I once witnessed mentors of mine spontaneously jumping into a frigid lake together, fully clothed, in response to daring each other to do so. New memories and enlivening sensory experiences are always available in nature, from taking a chilly walk in the snow to swimming in the ocean. When couples immerse themselves in the sensory experiences of nature, communication tends to open up in the process.

Communicate Openly

Open, honest communication is the foundation of long-term, committed relationships that thrive. If you find that you and your partner are out of sync, communicate your feelings in the most specific and vulnerable terms possible while offering a potential path forward. "I feel disconnected from you lately and would like to spend more time together this week" is an example of open communication that helps meet a relationship's needs.

Sometimes couples hit an impasse in their relationship or the chasm of distance feels too wide to cross. These couples may benefit from the additional support of a therapist who can help facilitate open and honest dialogue. It's important to remember that it's never too early or too late to seek support through couples therapy. It doesn't indicate that a couple is in crisis or on the verge of a breakup—it indicates a responsible decision toward personal growth.

Rekindling your relationship with transparent communication is a healthy way to close a chapter of disconnection and create a new beginning. When couples commit to communicating openly and authentically, often the best is yet to come.

A NEW DAY

Ella and Shane were used to beating around the bush. "Where would you like to begin?" the therapist would ask at the start their sessions. Ella and Shane would often take turns encouraging the other to share, as if there were an open secret in the room.

To shake up the conversation, the therapist asked the couple to share some significant memories of feeling known, loved, safe, and afraid. At first, they stayed in their comfort zone, "That card you gave me on my birthday was nice," Shane said. "I felt loved ..."

But gradually, as they discussed feelings of safety and fear, the conversation got emotional.

"I'm not sure that I ever let go of fear from when you broke up with me early in our relationship," Shane shared, his voice breaking. "I know that was years ago, but I still think of it when you don't reply to a text message quickly or when you seem upset with me."

"Shane, I had no idea. I feel awful. What can I do to help?" Ella reached out, taking Shane's hand.

"I think if you would tell me when we have an issue in our relationship, it would help me feel safe. I feel like I have to guess most of the time," Shane reflected.

Thanking Shane for his self-observation and vulnerability, Ella scooted closer to him on the sofa. "I'm going to be more open, Shane. I know I've closed up a bit in the past few years. I'm committed to staying open with you now."

The therapist knew that Shane and Ella had turned a corner. Week after week, when the therapist reminded them of their renewed commitment to authenticity in their relationship, they let their guards down and shared their feelings. It was a new day in their relationship, and all it took was a simple choice toward connection.

Conclusion

Congratulations! You and your partner have taken the time to read this book and put in the work to cultivate a relationship that is set up to thrive. This alone points to your commitment.

Seeking additional resources to bond and tend to your relationship will allow you and your partner to sustain your growth. Consider taking a class, attending therapy together, or finding relationship mentors who can spur you and your partner toward a great future together.

My purpose in writing this book (and my personal vocation in life) has been to help couples thrive in their closest relationships. My hope is that you and your partner will be discerning and intentional about the kind of relationship you build together, using the practical strategies and applicable examples from this book to guide you. What's more important in life than relationships with the people closest to you? Deep meaning and purpose come from committed relationships—they are one of the greatest gifts. As I like to say to my clients, "I'm here for you, for better or for worse; let's make it better, together."

RESOURCES

CoupleCheckup.com
A research-based relationship inventory for couples who want to assess the strengths and challenges of their relationship.

Gottman.com
The world's foremost relationship researcher John Gottman's best-selling books and resources offer science-based methods for safeguarding relationships.

LesandLeslie.com
Dozens of best-selling relationship books; an assessment to help couples determine which conversations to prioritize as their relationship progresses.

Prepare-Enrich.com
A relationship inventory that links to couples therapy for couples who want to prepare their relationship for the future.

RelationshipsforBetter.com
The author's therapy private practice based near Los Angeles, California. Relationships for Better focuses on helping individuals and couples thrive in their closest relationships.

RestorationTherapyTraining.com
Trainings for relationship therapists and a nationwide directory of therapists who specialize in restoration therapy.

REFERENCES

Baumrind, Diana. "Child Care Practices Anteceding Three Patterns of Preschool Behavior," *Genet Psychol Monographs*, 75(1): 43–88 (February 1967). pubmed.ncbi.nlm.nih.gov/6032134.

Bilow, Rochelle. "Want Your Marriage to Last?" YourTango. November 18, 2013. yourtango.com/experts/rochelle-bilow/want-your-marriage-last.

Blakeslee, Sandra. "Tracing the Brain's Pathways for Linking Emotion and Reason." *New York Times*. December 6, 1994. nytimes.com/1994/12/06/science /tracing-the-brain-s-pathways-for-linking-emotion-and-reason.html.

Bowlby, John. *Attachment and Loss, Vol. 1.* London: The Hogarth Press and Institute of Psycho-Analysis, 1969.

Braithwaite, S. R., Edward A. Selby, and Frank D. Fincham. "Forgiveness and Relationship Satisfaction: Mediating Mechanisms." *Journal of Family Psychology*, 25(4), 2011: 551–559. doi.org/10.1037/a0024526.

Burton, Neel. "These Are the 7 Types of Love." *Psychology Today*. Revised April 27, 2020. psychologytoday.com/us/blog/hide-and-seek/201606/these -are-the-7-types-love.

Chapman, Gary. *The Five Love Languages: The Secret to Love That Lasts.* Chicago: Northfield Publishing, 2015.

Chartered Management Institute. "Setting SMART Objectives Checklist 231." managers.org.uk/wp-content/uploads/2020/03/CHK-231-Setting_Smart _Objectives.pdf.

Cloud, Henry, and John Townsend. *Boundaries: When to Say Yes, How to Say No to Take Control of Your Life.* Grand Rapids: Zondervan, 1992.

Debt.com. "Fewer Americans Are Budgeting in 2019 ---- Although They Think Everyone Else Should." PRNewswire. April 4, 2019. https://www.

prnewswire
.com/news-releases/fewer-americans-are-budgeting-in-2019—although-they
-think-everyone-else-should-300824384.html.

Drucker, Peter. *The Practice of Management.* London: Heinemann, 1955.

Gordon, Thomas. *Parent Effectiveness Training: The Proven Program for Raising Responsible Children.* New York: Harmony Books, 2000.

Gottman, John, and Nan Silver. *The Seven Principles for Making Marriage Work.* New York: Harmony, 2015.

Hargrave, Terry D., and Franz Pfitzer. *Restoration Therapy: Understanding and Guiding Healing in Marriage and Family Therapy.* Oxfordshire: Routledge, 2011.

Horne, Corrina. "Defining Your Family of Origin & How It Impacts You." BetterHelp. Updated November 23, 2020. betterhelp.com/advice/family /defining-your-family-of-origin-how-it-impacts-you.

Karremans, Johan C., Paul A. M. Van Lange, Jaap W. Ouwerkerk, and Esther S. Kluwer. "When Forgiving Enhances Psychological Well-Being: The Role of Interpersonal Commitment." *Journal of Personality and Social Psychology,* 84(5), 2003: 1011–1026. doi.org/10.1037/0022-3514.84.5.1011.

Langlais, Michael, and Siera Schwanz. "Religiosity and Relationship Quality of Dating Relationships: Examining Relationship Religiosity as a Mediator." *Religions* 8, no. 9, (August 2017). doi.org/10.3390/rel8090187.

Lapp, David. "Marriage Is a Community Affair." Institute for Family Studies. May 26, 2014. ifstudies.org/blog/marriage-is-a-community-affair.

Masci, David. "Shared Religious Beliefs in Marriage Important to Some, but Not All, Married Americans." Pew Research Center. October 27, 2016. pewresearch.org/fact-tank/2016/10/27/shared-religious-beliefs-in -marriage-important-to-some-but-not-all-married-americans.

Newman, Kira M. "What Playfulness Can Do for Your Relationship." *Greater Good Magazine*. February 11, 2020.

Olson, David H., Douglas H. Sprenkle, and Candyce S. Russell. "Circumplex Model of Marital and Family Systems: I. Cohesion and Adaptability Dimensions, Family Types, and Clinical Applications." *Family Process* 8, no. 1, April 1979. onlinelibrary.wiley.com/doi/abs/10.1111/j.1545-5300.1979.00003.x.

Parker-Pope, Tara. "Reinventing Date Night for Long-Married Couples." *New York Times*. February 12, 2008. nytimes.com/2008/02/12/health/12well.html.

Patterson, Kerry, Joseph Grenny, Ron McMillan, and Al Switzler. *Crucial Conversations: Tools for Talking When Stakes Are High*. New York: McGraw-Hill, 2002.

Perel, Esther. *Mating in Captivity: Unlocking Erotic Intelligence*. New York: HarperCollins, 2017.

Perel, Esther. "What Is Erotic Intelligence?" Mindvalley Talks. November 26, 2017. youtube.com/watch?v=tO0xgj3kEuI.

Prior, Vivien, and Dayna Glaser. *Child and Adolescent Mental Health Series. Understanding Attachment and Attachment Disorders: Theory, Evidence and Practice*. London: Jessica Kingsley Publishers, 2006.

U.S. Bureau of Labor. "National Longitudinal Surveys Frequently Asked Questions." Accessed January 5, 2021. https://www.bls.gov/nls/questions-and-answers.htm.

Whitebread, David, and Sue Bingham. "Habit Formation and Learning in Young Children." University of Cambridge, 2013. mascdn.azureedge.net/cms/mas-habit-formation-and-learning-in-young-children-executive-summary.pdf.

INDEX

A

Agape, 7
Altruism, 88
Apologizing, 103–104
Attachment theory, 28–34

B

Baumrind, Diana, 135
Body language, 60–62
Boundaries
  with family members, 137
  for intimacy, 82–84
  values and, 104–106
Bowlby, John, 21, 28

C

Careers
  expectations about, 119–121
  job loss, 121–122
  work/life balance, 124–125
Chapman, Gary, 13
Children, 128–134, 136
Closeness. *See* Intimacy
Cloud, Henry, 82
Commitment, 10–11, 144
Communication. *See also* Conflict resolution
  about privacy, 69
  active listening, 55, 58–59
  body language, 60–62
  clear, 59
  curiosity, 56
  of expectations, 65–66
  of goals, 67
  to improve physical connection, 76–78
  of insecurities, 66–67
  "I" statements, 59
  kindness in, 62–63
  relational requests, 70
  respect, 57
  specificity, 63
  stating the obvious, 63
  storytelling, 63–64
  technology and, 55–56
  trust, 69
  understanding, 68
  validation, 54
Community, 16–18
Conflict resolution
  apologizing, 103–104
  boundaries, 104–106
  communicating pain points, 92–93
  creative problem-solving, 102–103
  emotional regulation, 94–100
  forgiveness, 106
  intent vs. impact, 101–102
  nonjudgmentalness, 92
  physical regulation, 94
Cooperation, 10
Cultural heritages, 43–44

D

Drucker, Peter, 144

E

Educational decisions, 136
Emotional regulation, 94–100
Eros, 7
Expectations
  about intimacy, 75
  career, 119–121
  clarifying, 12
  communication, 65–66

F

Family
  adaptivity structures, 24–25
  blended, 131–132
  children, 128–131
  cohesiveness, 26–27
  cultural heritage, 43–44
  extended, 137–139
  fostering/adoption, 131–134
  of origin, 22–23, 28
  parenting, 135–136
  traditions and customs, 45–46
Finances
  banking, 114
  bill-paying, 114–116
  budgeting, 116–117
  debt, 116–117
  emotions around, 112
  long-term goals, 118–119
  spending and saving habits, 113–114
Five Love Languages, The (Chapman), 13
Forgiveness, 106
Four Steps technique, 95–100
Friendships, 139–140

G

Goals
  communication about, 67
  financial, 118–119
  SMART, 144–145
Gordon, Thomas, 59
Gottman, John, 4, 38
Gratitude, 85
Grounding, 84

H

Hargrave, Sharon, 95
Hargrave, Terry, 8, 95
Household chores, 122–124

I

Identities
  communal, 16–18
  individual, 4–5
  relationship, 8
Insecurities, 66–67, 86–87, 92–93
Intimacy
  altruism, 88
  boundaries, 82–84
  dates, 79–80
  emotional, 80
  fantasies, 82
  gratitude, 85
  physical connection, 76–78
  playfulness, 81
  prioritizing joy, 86–87
  risk-taking, 85
  and self-worth, 88
  time for, 78–79
  trust, 74–75

L

Lapp, David, 16
Love languages, 13–15
Love styles, 7
Ludus, 7

M

Miscommunication, 68. *See also* Communication
Mission statements, 46–47

N

Neural pathways, 21, 22, 93

O

Olson's Circumplex Model, 23

P

Parenting styles, 135–136
Parrott, Les and Leslie, 79
Perel, Esther, 4, 81
Phileo, 7
Political beliefs, 41–43
Pragma, 7
Privacy, 69

Q

Questions
  avoiding overuse of "why," 62
  open-ended, 5–6

R

Reconnecting, 145–149
Religious and spiritual beliefs, 39–41
Runaway Bride (film), 4

S

Self-worth, 88
*Seven Principles for Making Marriage
    Work* (Gottman), 4
Sex. *See* Intimacy
Storge, 7

T

Traditions and customs, 45–46
Trust
  in commitment, 144
  communicating, 69
  demonstrating, 74–75
Two Truths and a Lie, 7

U

"Us-ness," 8–9

V

Values, 38–39, 104–106
Vulnerability, 85, 86–87, 92–93

W

Whitaker, Carl, 8
Work/life balance, 124–125